If Your Adolescent Has Autism

Daniel Romer, PhD, Director of Research

The Adolescent Mental Health Initiative of the Annenberg Public Policy Center and the Sunnylands Trust

---

Patrick E. Jamieson, PhD, series editor

Other books in the series

If Your Adolescent Has Schizophrenia
Raquel E. Gur, MD, and Ann Braden Johnson, PhD

If Your Adolescent Has an Anxiety Disorder
Edna B. Foa, PhD, and Linda Wasmer Andrews

If Your Adolescent Has ADHD
Thomas J. Power, PhD, and Linda Wasmer Andrews

If Your Adolescent Has an Eating Disorder
B. Timothy Walsh, MD, and Deborah R. Glasofer, PhD

If Your Adolescent Has Bipolar Disorder
Dwight L. Evans, MD, Tami D. Benton, MD,
and Katherine Ellison

If Your Adolescent Has Depression
Dwight L. Evans, MD, Moira A. Rynn, MD,
and Katherine Ellison

If Your Adolescent Has Autism

An Essential Resource for Parents

Emily J. Willingham, PhD
With a foreword by Susan W. White, PhD

THE ANNENBERG
PUBLIC POLICY CENTER
OF THE UNIVERSITY OF PENNSYLVANIA

The Adolescent Mental Health Initiative of the Annenberg
Public Policy Center and the Sunnylands Trust

The Annenberg Foundation Trust at
SUNNYLANDS

OXFORD
UNIVERSITY PRESS

OXFORD
UNIVERSITY PRESS

Oxford University Press is a department of the University of Oxford.
It furthers the University's objective of excellence in research, scholarship,
and education by publishing worldwide. Oxford is a registered trademark of
Oxford University Press in the UK and in certain other countries.

Published in the United States of America by Oxford University Press
198 Madison Avenue, New York, NY 10016, United States of America.

© Oxford University Press 2025

All rights reserved. No part of this publication may be reproduced, stored in a retrieval
system, transmitted, used for text and data mining, or used for training artificial
intelligence, in any form or by any means, without the prior permission in writing of
Oxford University Press, or as expressly permitted by law, by license, or under terms agreed
with the appropriate reprographics rights organization. Inquiries concerning reproduction
outside the scope of the above should be sent to the Rights Department, Oxford University
Press, at the address above.

You must not circulate this work in any other form
and you must impose this same condition on any acquirer.

Library of Congress Cataloging-in-Publication Data

Names: Willingham, Emily Jane, 1968– author
Title: If your adolescent has autism : an essential resource for parents /
Emily J. Willingham, PhD ; with a foreword by Susan W. White, PhD.
Description: New York, NY : Oxford University Press, [2025] |
Series: Adolescent mental health initiative | Includes bibliographical references and index.
Identifiers: LCCN 2025017137 (print) | LCCN 2025017138 (ebook) |
ISBN 9780197513149 (hardback) | ISBN 9780197513132 (paperback) |
ISBN 9780197513163 epub | ISBN 9780197817032
Subjects: LCSH: Parents of autistic children |
Autistic children | Child rearing
Classification: LCC HQ773.8 .W57 2025 (print) | LCC HQ773.8 (ebook) |
DDC 649/.154—dc23/eng/20250616
LC record available at https://lccn.loc.gov/2025017137
LC ebook record available at https://lccn.loc.gov/2025017138

DOI: 10.1093/oso/9780197513149.001.0001

Paperback Printed by Marquis Book Printing, Canada
Hardback Printed by Bridgeport National Bindery, Inc., United States of America

The manufacturer's authorized representative in the EU for product safety is Oxford
University Press España S.A., Parque Empresarial San Fernando de Henares, Avenida de
Castilla, 2 – 28830 Madrid (www.oup.es/en or product.safety@oup.com). OUP España
S.A. also acts as importer into Spain of products made by the manufacturer.

Contents

Foreword   vii

Introduction: New Challenges in the Teenage Years   1

One
Autism and Adolescence: An Overview   9

Two
The Secondary School Years   29

Three
Autism and Co-occurring
   Genetic and Medical Conditions   56

Four
Autism and Co-occurring Mental
   Health and Behavioral Conditions   80

Five
Autism, Adolescence, and Social Connections   105

Six
Puberty and Hygiene   136

Seven
Autism, Adolescence, and Sexuality   152

Eight
Transition From High School   173

Glossary   203
Resources   208
Bibliography   214
Index   229

Foreword

Parents of autistic teens who are searching for a reader-friendly resource with targeted direction and sound advice can stop looking. Few (OK, likely *no*) parents of adolescents talk about how incredibly easy and stress free it is to raise teenagers. As your child undergoes their lengthy and nonlinear metamorphosis into a more or less independent adult, you as the parent experience all the excitement, the firsts, and the inevitable challenges right alongside them. All this applies for parents who are raising a teen who is on the autism spectrum, but in the context of a disorder that is usually lifelong, though constantly changing with respect to its presentation and associated challenges. Historically, most resources for parents and other loved ones have been built around topics like early identification, early intervention, socialization during childhood, and other experiences and challenges specific to autism spectrum disorder during the preteen years. *If Your Adolescent Has Autism* is a resource for family members of teens and adults on the spectrum, including those who have been recently diagnosed.

As the rate of diagnosis of autism has increased steadily over the past several years, so has awareness of the fact that most autistic kids grow into autistic teenagers and eventually autistic adults. The disorder is not confined to childhood. Parents of teens on the spectrum are many in number, but often isolated in experience and in their community. There are many reasons for this, and one that is often felt acutely during the teen years is that these parents don't have the seemingly "ready-made" social networks that many of their peers do, supported by activities and organizations like parent associations, sports boosters, athletic events, and after-school activities. The disconnection from peers that many, though not all, autistic teens experience is felt by their parents, by extension. If nothing else, please consider this book a reminder that you are *not* alone in this. One of my favorite quotes (source unknown) is, "Be kind to everyone. You never know if they have a teenager at home."

For people with autism, adolescence is an especially vulnerable phase of life. There are social as well as neurobiological reasons for this, borne out by the research. The neural reorganization, heightened hormone activity, and increasing social demands of adolescence can interfere with a person's ability to learn and apply the skills needed for success. Research on developmental changes in physiological responding indicates that, during adolescence, many autistic youth experience increased reactivity and heightened risk for social stress. Adaptive functioning, or skill acquisition, does not keep pace with chronological age, such that teens are often further behind their age-mates, and new mental health problems often emerge during adolescence. Research suggests that parents can be instrumental in helping their autistic teens develop healthy identities that are more accepting of neurodiversity. Parents and other family members play a vital role in the lives of their autistic teen.

If Your Adolescent Has Autism is filled with rich content and balanced perspectives written in a readily digestible way, along with extremely helpful resource suggestions and case material. For example, there is consideration of social discourse and balancing "wanting the best for your child" with "acceptance of them as a unique person" (Chapter 5). A whole chapter is dedicated to intimacy and sexuality, topics often overlooked in parent resources. This book provides very detailed information on parental rights, educational and disability law, and how parents can build on their child's strengths (Chapters 2 and 8). Finally, common parent concerns related to mental health, including self-harm and treatment options, are addressed. The breadth of content is truly impressive.

Susan W. White, PhD
Professor and Doddridge Saxon Chairholder
in Clinical Psychology
Department of Psychology
Associate Dean of Research, College of Arts and Sciences
The University of Alabama

Introduction

New Challenges in the Teenage Years

Most people would agree that adolescence can be a tough time for parents and their teens. Autistic teenagers may face specific challenges, though, and need targeted support from the adults in their lives to take advantage of their strengths and help them fulfill their potential. The road ahead can be challenging for parents and caregivers, too, especially because the teenage years can involve surprising changes in a child, as well as in society's expectations of them.

Most books for parents of autistic children focus on the early years and offer limited information about adolescence and young adulthood. This book is different. It presents the latest in scientifically supported information about what happens when autism and adolescence intersect. I cover the teen years, largely focusing on middle school (sometimes called junior high school) and high school, along with the transition from high school into adulthood and, where relevant, college and employment.

If you love a young autistic person, this book will provide information and guidance you both can trust, presented with compassion and understanding and an emphasis on both the strengths and the challenges of having autism. In these pages, you will find the real-life stories of autistic people and parents and caregivers like you, along with essential information presented in terms that are easy to understand. At the end of this book is a section titled "Resources," divided by chapter number, that contains additional resources you can turn to for more tools and support to help you and your autistic child have the best possible experience on this path to adulthood.

Who Wrote This Book and Why

Dr. Emily J. Willingham has authored several books, including the *Complete Idiot's Guide to College Biology*, *The Informed Parent: A Science-Based Resource for Your Child's First Four Years*, and *The Tailored Brain: From Ketamine, to Keto, to Companionship, a User's Guide to Feeling Better and Thinking Smarter*. She holds a doctorate in developmental biology, has a quarter century of experience working with adolescents, has held several academic appointments at major universities, and is a veteran science journalist. She has extensive experience living with, working with, and writing about autistic people.

What You Will Find in This Book

Chapter One—Autism and adolescence: an overview

In many ways, an autistic teenager is going to be just like any other teenager. Autistic people are not all the same, of course, and disposition, environment, genetics unrelated to autism, and the usual teenage struggles will differ for each person. But some common themes and issues arise with the combination of adolescence and autism, with specific needs emerging related to this complex, often difficult, and sometimes thrilling stage of life. Because autistic people develop in ways and at rates that may vary from typical development, it is important for parents and caregivers to know that some major milestones may occur later than expected.

Chapter one offers a few stories of autistic teenagers with different trajectories and levels of disability before getting into the details of how autism spectrum disorder is diagnosed. You will also learn about the prevalence of autism, why these numbers have increased in recent decades, and what experts think about the underlying causes. After a brief look at controversies related to an autism diagnosis and why an autistic teenager would benefit from having a formal diagnosis, the chapter closes with a short discussion about co-occurring conditions.

Chapter Two—The secondary school years

The years spanning secondary school (middle school or junior high school and high school, for most children) will bring considerable change for almost any child, and autistic children are no exception. Development for autistic children may move forward in fits and starts and not according to the "typical" path. Autistic students may need extra academic and social supports, with one or the other being more essential depending on disability level and support needs. Mixing social and academic pressures during a time when both become more intense and complex can be especially difficult for autistic teens.

In Chapter two you will find useful information about what supports can look like in and out of the classroom, how to construct a school day that doesn't overwhelm your autistic teen, and the ins and outs of formal supports available within schools, such as the Individualized Education Program. The chapter also features stories and feedback from autistic people about both what they found to be beneficial during these school years and what caused them to struggle the most.

Chapter Three—Autism and co-occurring genetic and medical conditions

The changes of puberty can sometimes unmask or worsen conditions that often accompany autism, including medical and psychiatric disorders. This chapter explains some of the science behind these associations with medical conditions, including epilepsy, joint hypermobility, gastrointestinal disorders, and genetic conditions, along with warning signs and interventions.

Co-occurring medical conditions are common among autistic people, and because these conditions can intensify or change during the teen years, parents must be alert to relevant signals. For each co-occurring condition I address in this chapter, I give an overview of its causes, associations with autism, signs and symptoms, and the role that changes in adolescence may play.

Chapter Four—Autism and co-occurring mental health and behavioral conditions

Autistic people have a higher likelihood of experiencing mental health–related and behavioral conditions, including attention-deficit/hyperactivity disorder, anxiety, mood disorders, and intellectual disability. Although these diagnoses can overlap with and share similar causes with the medical conditions covered in the previous chapter, the risk that a person's autism will mask another diagnosis—known as *diagnostic overshadowing*—may be greater for mental health disorders.

In Chapter four, you will learn about the most common co-occurring mental health and behavioral/developmental conditions, especially those that may arise or intensify in the teen years. The chapter covers how attention-deficit/hyperactivity disorder, depression, anxiety, and others may interact with and overlap with the features of autism, leading to diagnostic confusion or overshadowing. Also included in this chapter are discussions of eating disorders, suicidality, and sleep problems, all of which are more likely to occur during adolescence. The chapter closes with a discussion of violence and autistic people, making the important, scientifically supported point that autistic people are far more likely to be targets of violence than to commit it.

Chapter Five—Autism, adolescence, and social connections

Adolescence comes with a lot of social baggage, and autistic teenagers can find the experience overwhelming. Understanding how a maturing autistic child experiences these changes and the best approaches to offering support is crucial for parents looking to help their child through this period.

A great deal of effort goes into helping autistic children "fit in" and gain "social skills" that will help them navigate the increasingly socially complicated world around them. This stage of life is a fast-moving conveyor belt of social experiences, which also means it is peak time for the many stumbles and pitfalls that come with learning the nuances of social interactions.

In Chapter five, you will learn about why becoming a "social thinker" is important for a teen, the obstacles autistic teens may encounter in developing this ability, and how to support them in moving past these obstacles. The chapter also features sections on navigating social media, friendships and dating, and bullying, all unavoidable parts of being a teen in the 21st century.

Chapter Six—*Puberty and hygiene*

A teenager with autism may not navigate some activities of daily living as easily as their typically developing peers, but that doesn't mean they never will. What many autistic teens will need, however, is guidance that builds on tools they already use to learn, step by step, how to understand and manage some of the more sensitive elements of puberty.

Issues around puberty and sexuality (covered in Chapter seven) may be among the most difficult for parents and teens to work through together. Chapter six offers numerous tips and strategies for you to use with your teen in developing practical approaches to dealing with things like personal hygiene changes and other experiences of puberty.

Chapter Seven—*Autism, adolescence, and sexuality*

The vast majority of adults engage in sexual activity during their lifetimes, and autistic people are no exception. The best way to ensure that sexuality and sex-related behaviors are healthy, safe, and fulfilling is to provide clear, scientifically supported information about this central aspect of life. If you find discussions of puberty difficult, ensuring that your child is appropriately informed about sexuality and sex may feel even more awkward. But doing so prepares young people to use safe, healthy practices that will support good quality of life into adulthood.

Chapter seven candidly presents issues related to sexuality and having autism, including how to communicate about consent—giving and receiving—and establishing boundaries. You will learn why sexuality education is as much about safety and protection as it is about specific anatomy.

This chapter also provides information about lesbian, gay, bisexual, transgender, queer, intersex, asexual, and others sexuality, including that of people who are asexual, because there is considerable overlap between these two populations and conventional sexuality education may exclude them. I realize that these subjects can be difficult for parents to broach with their child, but a crucial role of parents is preparing their kids for adulthood. The information in this chapter will support you in equipping your teen with tools they will need for a lifetime.

Chapter Eight—Transition from high school

The final chapter of this book focuses on planning for a moment that every adolescent will eventually reach: the transition to adulthood and which path your teen will take as an adult. As momentous as this may feel, no single choice must be permanent, and this chapter covers a flexible approach to preparing for the "services cliff" that awaits when an autistic person turns 18 (or 21, depending on their high school program).

This wide-ranging chapter touches on many things parents should consider as part of this planning, including legal issues, housing, employment, continuing education, support services, wellness and healthcare, and money management. The common theme of this chapter—and indeed of this book—is that for autistic teenagers, the key words are *self-determination* and *self-advocacy*. Self-determination means that young people are as well-equipped as possible to make their own decisions based on the options available to them. Self-advocacy means that they are as equipped as possible to make their desires and needs known.

Because transitioning from high school into the early adult years requires consideration of every single aspect of life, the material in this chapter could comprise a whole book on its own, so as with other chapters, I include a resource list of excellent, thorough, and detailed guides on transition planning for autistic teens, which is at the end of this book (Resources). At every step, including your autistic young person in decisions and encouraging their self-determination and self-advocacy are in themselves essential elements of this preparation.

Chapter One

Autism and Adolescence

An Overview

Adolescence, regardless of who is going through it, is a time of transition and transformation. It tends to overlap with puberty, when a person physically develops into an adult, but the stage of adolescence lasts well beyond the physical changes of puberty. Humans are complex organisms and they undergo a multitude of changes from head to toe during this phase of development. A main feature of this stage of life is the growing need for independence, but many teens entering this stage also want stability, support, and guidance.

Here, I usually refer to people undergoing adolescence as *teens* because that's the age I associate most with this stage of life. But research suggests that, on average, adolescence starts in the preteens and can last into the mid-20s. For people who are developing at their own rate, possibly different from what is typical, this time frame can shift. The shifts usually mean arriving at certain milestones, such as driving a car, at a later age, but they can also mean that some phases of adolescence last a little longer. Although autistic people often experience a journey in their development that's different from what is typical, as it is for everyone else, that journey is always moving forward.

Key experiences of adolescence include forming social attachments independently, learning to navigate a complicated world, and gaining the tools to make choices and determine their own fate as fully as possible. The role of the parent, guardian, or caregiver in this process can be difficult and can fluctuate daily; caring adults must seek an appropriate balance between being a "safe" place and stepping back to give a young person the space they need to grow into an adult.

Many of the changes of adolescence coincide with areas in which autistic young people may experience the greatest difficulties. The complexities of human social communications can become especially tangled during the high school years as teens figure out social dynamics, community, and self-understanding. The core features of autism can include difficulty tracking these complicated interactions and "reading between the lines," especially with nonverbal communication. Because of these difficulties, this period can be especially challenging on the social front.

The main theme of this book is planning and preparation. With the right tools, parents and autistic teens can mindfully work together with a support community of friends, teachers, and others to address areas where an autistic young person might struggle most. A parent's role will likely change from moment to moment throughout this time frame, but one constant will be that parents should always have the goal of equipping their child with tools for making their own decisions, managing their own daily lives, and advocating for their own needs.

Snapshots of Autistic Teens

Anderson

When he entered middle school, Anderson[1] shifted from being homeschooled to attending a small, traditional classroom. Although Anderson did well academically, he made no friends and declared little interest in being friends with any of the people in his class. His parents took him at his word and didn't pressure him or try to organize social experiences for him.

Anderson did make a few friends in high school. The "glue" for him was sports team participation and academic competition with other students. But even with this crew, he always maintained a distance. He tended to decline social invitations to typical teen activities, like going to movies, hanging out, or dating. In fact, he had no interest in romantic involvement and expressed confusion about why his peers did have such interests. As he progressed through school, he excelled and was well liked among both peers and faculty. After graduation, though, he had almost no contact with any of his friends from high school. He preferred to pursue his interests on his own and to spend time only with his family.

Anderson chose to attend a university near his parents' home. During his time in college, he experienced a prolonged depression and intense anxiety that was much worse than his prior lifelong experiences with social anxiety. Looking back, he says he thought that the triggers for these episodes were probably an overwhelming course schedule and some trouble planning his time each day. He also had migraines during this time. Anderson says that he learned from this months-long

---

[1] Not his real name. Throughout this book, I use pseudonyms for people whose stories I feature to protect their privacy.

episode that he has limits he needs to respect, or there will be consequences.

Candace

Candace, who grew up during the later 20th century, didn't know as a teen that she was autistic. "I wish I had known," she says. She also wishes she'd been homeschooled and had grown up in a home where the adults didn't fight with each other constantly. Her way of coping was to "escape into books," she told me. During her teen years, "helicopter parenting" mostly didn't exist, which meant Candace was on her own a lot. She ended up spending her time in nature, which eased her tension and provided an escape from her struggles. But without understanding what made her feel different from others and with no tools for understanding why she felt that way, she says, "Most of my adolescence was awful."

The Twins

Augmentative and alternative communication tools are available to those who find speaking difficult or impossible. These tools may translate typing into voice, for example. But they are also controversial. Some of these tools rely on support from another person, who might, for example, move a letterboard around as an autistic person chooses letters to spell words. The transition of paper letterboards to digital formats, such as use of a tablet that can be propped up, has reduced some of this controversy because autistic users manage the entire process themselves. One parent of twin sons, aged 19, discussed the effects of this new technology in an interview with the family's local newspaper.

Both young men were nonspeaking. As they grew, no one replaced their baby books with books for older readers, and their parents didn't realize that the twins had advanced beyond early reading levels. When the young men were able to communicate using an iPad keyboard, they let their parent know that they wanted books for older readers. In fact, they requested books in specific subject areas, such as space.

Until they could use these digital assisted communication tools to self-advocate for their interests, no one was aware of them. As with any teenager, when nonspeaking autistic children enter adolescence, many things can change, including their interests. They may also shift from nonspeaking to semispeaking or speaking. Many unexpected things await any child entering the teen years, autistic or not.

Hayden

Hayden is a nonspeaking autistic young man who has developed many sports-related skills, in part thanks to support from his father. Hayden's father, who shared their story with the United Kingdom's National Autistic Society, says that sports began with swimming when Hayden was little, because Hayden loved water. The boy soon also began riding horses as a weekly therapy, and by the time he reached his teens, he had become quite skilled both at riding horses and at swimming. Hayden also began working out with his father at the gym.

In addition to using an app called Proloquo2Go on his iPad to make his needs known, Hayden also speaks using short phrases, such as "Let's go," to convey that he's done with an activity. His entry into adolescence has involved building skills, engaging in his interests, and finding new ones. In the process, he is also expanding his communication tools. Each of these signs of progress is an important part of everyone's transition to adulthood.

Although these young people are living their lives in different ways from one another, they all have one thing in common: They are autistic. That means that even if their developmental paces vary, they have certain features of behavior and communication in common. In the following sections of this chapter, I give an overview of those features as they are formally described and diagnosed by people in the medical and mental health communities, discuss how commonly autism occurs and why the numbers keep changing, and touch on some of the science around what causes autism (and related controversies). I close this overview with a note on important considerations around language and what to expect from this book.

The Question of Getting a Diagnosis

When talking about being an autistic teen, autistic people describe a huge range of experiences. Some, like Candace, felt that it was "hell." Others came through it OK, supported by family and finding friends with shared interests. Still others spent their adolescence as undiagnosed autistic teens. That experience left many of them feeling confused about why they just didn't seem to click with their peers or why they felt detached from some of the intense social urges so many other teens experience.

Regardless, for many it was not simply having autism that caused the unpleasant experiences or hell of middle school and high school. Their misery came from how their peers (and sometimes the adults around them) treated or reacted to them. One autistic adult, looking back on their time in high school, wished that they'd "been able to tell the difference between people who liked me and people who wanted something from me." Another "desperately" wished they'd known that they had autism and "that what I was experiencing was not the universal norm."

If you can remember your own middle school or high school years, a lot of what these individuals describe may sound familiar. Like most teens, autistic adults report that in their adolescence, they just wanted to understand their place in the world and find others like them. Most of us can relate to this, but one thing that emerges often from stories of the autistic teen experience is that not knowing about their autism made everything worse. That's one of many reasons that understanding what the features of autism are and recognizing them in an adolescent can be crucial. This awareness is especially important for autistic girls, who can have significant delays in diagnosis because what we know about autism is based mostly on studies in boys (Kanfiszer et al., 2017), though this is starting to change.

For other adolescents, however, the autism "label" is something they want to keep private or even reject (Mogenson & Mason, 2015). As with all possible identities they may bear, teens may engage in extensive negotiation around how much or how little they want to reveal or embrace. Working through who we are and how we identify is a common adolescent experience. As such, the question of whether to proactively seek a diagnosis during childhood is complicated.

The Shifting Landscape of Diagnosis

A publication known as the *Diagnostic and Statistical Manual of Mental Disorders*, fifth edition (the *DSM-5* for short), details the diagnostic criteria for autism spectrum disorder; its most recent edition was published in 2013 and it was updated in 2021 (known as the *DSM-5-TR* for short). When the *DSM-5* was originally published in 2013, its description of the autism diagnosis was controversial. The new version not only blended what had previously been separate subcategories (autism spectrum disorder, pervasive developmental disorder not otherwise specified, and Asperger's disorder) but also created a new category: social communication disorder (National Autistic Society).

Some experts and advocates predicted that because of these changes, autistic people would not receive the correct diagnosis (Reichow & Volkmar, 2018) and instead be shifted into the less understood and more vaguely defined "social communication disorder" category. The change in these categories "narrows what constitutes the condition to the point of leaving out individuals at the edges of the spectrum," wrote experts Brian Reichow and Fred Volkmar in an opinion piece. The worry was that the changes in the *DSM-5* would mean that fewer people would "qualify" for a diagnosis of autism and thus would not receive the services they needed.

Since the social communication disorder category was established, some studies have borne out these concerns. According to one report, most children who met the criteria for social communication disorder also scored high on certain measures strongly linked to autism (Flax et al., 2019). The researchers concluded that children in this group might be overlooked if they were tested only for a social communication disorder and wouldn't receive the services they need for having autism.

Research conducted in the 5 years after the new category was established (Kulage et al., 2020) confirmed these concerns. The number of autism diagnoses fell during those 5 years. Some people would have been diagnosed as having autism using the earlier autism criteria, but were not according to the most recent version. This excluded group might not receive the supports they needed. The authors of one study concluded that the need for social communication disorder as an alternative diagnosis to autism "is unclear" (Flax et al., 2019, p. 3).

The 2021 update to the *DSM-5* also made changes to the autism criteria for social communication and interaction. The update involves a change to the language around one of the criteria lists, known as Criterion A. The lead-in to the list originally read, "as manifested by the following." This phrasing was changed in the *DSM-5-TR* to "as manifested by *all* of the following" (American Psychological Association, 2022). That small addition of the word "all" had a big impact—it meant that all three elements of Criterion A were now required for a diagnosis. These three elements are deficits or impairments in

- social-emotional reciprocity,
- nonverbal communicative behaviors used for social interaction, and
- developing, maintaining, and understanding relationships.

These elements are also among the most important areas of growth during the adolescent period. Requiring all three to be present for a diagnosis now means that fewer people will be formally diagnosed with autism.

The 2021 update to the *DSM-5* also included a small change in how clinicians describe conditions that might be associated with autism. The 2013 version read "associated with another neurodevelopmental, mental or behavioral disorder." The updated version reads "associated with another neurodevelopmental, mental or behavioral problem." The reason for this change is that not all co-occurring conditions are called disorders (Hess, 2022). This book looks at some of these co-occurring conditions in more detail in two later chapters.

Diagnostic Criteria

The diagnostic criteria for autism, as they are given in the *DSM-5*, include five categories (A, B, C, D, and E). Criteria A and B each have a sublisting that gives more detail.

Criterion A

Criterion A concerns problems ("deficits"; the quotation marks are mine because what constitutes a deficit depends on context and perspective) with social communication and social interaction across several contexts, listing three elements, as described previously: deficits in social-emotional reciprocity; nonverbal communicative behaviors used for social interaction; and developing, maintaining, and understanding relationships.

Examples of deficits in social-emotional reciprocity (social and emotional "give and take") include approaching other people in an atypical way, such as skipping conversational openings and talking right away about a key interest. Another example might be making limited or no response to an attempt at social interaction from another person.

Deficits in nonverbal communicative behaviors may include facial expressions that others find hard to interpret or atypical body language. For the relationships element, examples include difficulty adjusting behavior to social context, such as lowering one's voice in a very quiet place, or showing little interest in connecting with peers.

A diagnostician would be expected to rate the "severity" of each of these elements. This rating is based on how much support the autistic person might need to accommodate their disability.

Criterion B

Criterion B concerns the core feature of engaging in "restricted, repetitive patterns of behavior, interests, or activities." Four elements are listed with this criterion:

- stereotyped or repetitive motor movements, such as echolalia (repeating heard phrases) or lining up toys;
- insistence on sameness/inflexibility/rigidity/ritualized patterns, exhibiting distress with apparently small changes, trouble with transitions, or wanting to eat the same thing every day;
- highly restricted interests with an "abnormal" intensity or focus (such as a "strong attachment" to "unusual objects"); and
- either heightened or subdued reactions to sensory information (such as not registering pain as expected or high sensitivity to certain sounds) or "unusual" interest in sensory aspects of the environment (such as a fascination with lights).

Again, the clinician is also expected to rate the severity of each of these elements. Again, the quotation marks used are mine because what constitutes abnormal or unusual depends on context and perspective.

Criteria C, D, and E

The last three criteria—C, D, and E—relate to

- timing of appearance of autistic features (early in development, Criterion C),

- significant functional impairment because of the features (Criterion D), and
- a lack of another better explanation for the features (Criterion E).

Clinicians must also consider whether there may be any intellectual impairment or other medical, genetic, or neurodevelopmental conditions and note the presence of any language impairment.

People diagnosed as having autism before 2021, when these latest criteria were published (i.e., those who have a "well-established" diagnosis based on previous *DSM* criteria), are still considered to have autism.

Sidebar: Social Communication Disorder Criteria

According to the authors of the *DSM-5-TR*, the social communication disorder diagnosis is to be considered for people with social communication difficulties who need supports but who do not meet the criteria for autism spectrum disorder. Four diagnostic criteria are listed for this condition (A, B, C, D). Criterion A lists four elements, each of which is associated with the other criteria:

- deficits in using communication for social purposes,
- impaired ability to shift communication to fit context,
- trouble following the "rules" of conversation (such as turn-taking), and
- difficulty "reading between the lines" and understanding conversational tactics such as humor or metaphors.

These deficits must result in functional limitations on communication and related activities (Criterion B), be present at an early age (Criterion C), and not result from some other cause (Criterion D).

Diagnostics and Diagnostic Delay

Some parents whose undiagnosed child might have autism may wonder whether exploring a diagnosis will be helpful or harmful. Anecdotal evidence and informal surveys suggest that autistic adults who endured adolescence not knowing about their autism almost uniformly express regret. "Knowing I was different earlier would have helped," one says. "I didn't begin to realize other people's brains worked differently until I was 22." Another said that they wished they had "known that I was neurodivergent and that what I was experiencing was not in fact the universal norm." Those who did know that they had autism largely report that the knowledge was helpful.

An autism diagnosis is possible as early as age 2 (and researchers are working on diagnosing autism in infancy; Clairmont et al., 2022). The average age at diagnosis tends to be later, however, usually after a child starts preschool or grade school (Mandy et al., 2022). Members of some groups tend to be diagnosed later than average, especially girls and children of color. Because of this lag, these young people risk living with confusion and feelings of isolation; they will also go without the accommodations and supports they need.

The level of supports needed can determine how early a diagnosis is made. Children diagnosed at a younger age tend to have more intense social, emotional, and behavioral difficulties because more obvious signs of autism tend to draw the attention of educators and other adults early on. Autistic children diagnosed at older ages tend to score higher on intelligence quotient (IQ) testing, be female, and have mothers with higher education levels (Mandy et al., 2022). Black children tend to be diagnosed later. In contrast to findings for White children, Black children who score lower on IQ testing and have more intense symptoms may be *more* likely to be diagnosed at a later age (Habayeb et al., 2022).

Prevalence

Estimates of how commonly autism occurs bear out these differences with regard to which autistic children are diagnosed and when. The U.S. Centers for Disease Control and Prevention (CDC) assesses the prevalence of autism by taking a kind of snapshot of 8-year-old U.S. children every 2 years. Since the year 2000, the numbers of children diagnosed with autism have risen steadily upward. This increase is overwhelmingly attributed to greater recognition—more people know about autism and recognize its features—and to diagnostic shifts, with a reduction in intellectual disability diagnoses going hand in hand with the increase in autism diagnoses.

In 2021, the CDC reported on its 2018 data (Maenner et al., 2021), giving an autism prevalence of 1 in 44 children in the United States. Globally, the estimated prevalence is about 1% to 2%, or 1–2 in 100 children.

Other researchers using different government data reported a prevalence of 3.14% across children and adolescents for 2019 and 2020 (Li et al., 2022), in agreement with a meticulous study done in Korea a few years ago (Kim et al., 2011). Other studies have reported prevalences ranging from 2.3% to 2.5% or so, including another analysis based on yet another U.S. data set that showed a 2020 prevalence of 2.7% (Li & He, 2022). Reports from elsewhere around the world reflect a similar variation and range, with researchers concluding that differences in diagnostic and healthcare practices also play a role.

An autism diagnosis is far more common among boys than among girls (most analyses include only two genders)—about

4.2 times as common, according to the CDC. However, that ratio has been shifting gradually with the recognition that autism in girls may look different (Andrews et al., 2021) and be more difficult to identify.

For example, giving highly focused attention to specific interests is common among autistic people. For girls, that attention may be focused on subjects that are seen as more "socially acceptable," such as horses. Girls might also show repetitive behaviors or line up toys, but their choice of toy might make these behaviors go unnoticed. Researchers have suggested that girls may be better at observing the social behaviors of others and able to "camouflage" their own behaviors that seem different.

The CDC has also broken down autism prevalence by ancestry and ethnicity (Maenner et al., 2021). At some of the agency's study sites, prevalences are lower among Hispanic and Black children compared with White children. CDC researchers found more intellectual disability diagnoses among autistic Black children compared with other groups. In addition, prevalence varies with how wealthy a family is (Winter et al., 2020), but not in a consistent pattern.

Regarding autistic adults, as of 2017, the CDC estimated a prevalence of about 2.21%, or more than 5 million people (CDC, 2017) in the United States. An autism diagnosis tends to be stable through a lifetime, with some exceptions. About a fifth of autistic children who score in the average or higher IQ range may no longer meet diagnostic criteria at age 25 (Elias & Lord, 2022). Other research has shown that the features of autism can fluctuate in intensity through life. They may ease up a bit from adolescence to midlife, but increase again with older age (Hong et al., 2023). Each individual autistic person will have their own experience through life.

Causes and Controversies

The increase in autism prevalence in the 21st century has triggered a search for causes—along with a lot of controversy. For many, the purpose of identifying one or more causes of autism has been to target these factors to reduce autism prevalence. For autistic people (and their allies) who see autism as part of their identity and their existence as a human right, these aims are considered bigotry against people with disabilities, known as ableism. They reject the idea that autism is something to be "fixed" or "eliminated."

Nevertheless, millions of dollars have been spent in the search for environmental factors that may contribute to autism. There are claims that everything from pesticides to vaccines are responsible. Decades of data point directly at our genes as the biggest influence, however.

Dozens and dozens of gene variants are thought to be candidates in autistic brain development (Rankin Willsey et al., 2022). Studies of twins highlight the powerful role of genetic similarity in sharing an autism diagnosis. Studies of nontwin siblings show increased odds that a child will have autism if they have an autistic sibling.

Once a child is diagnosed as having autism, other family members may come to recognize autistic traits in themselves, though they may not meet the formal diagnostic criteria for autism or feel that they have autism. One term for this is the *broad autism phenotype* (a phenotype is the observable result of a gene's activity). It's extremely common for family members to learn more about themselves or others after an autistic child is diagnosed.

Experts estimate that genes contribute anywhere from 80% to 95% of the development of the autistic brain. Genes likely guide how the brain is built well before birth. This powerful role of genetics in neurodevelopment (the development of the brain) is known not just for autism but also for other conditions, like attention-deficit/hyperactivity disorder.

Yet, there is still a place for environmental factors in how autism develops, including a "background effect" from other genes. Although the common perception of "environment" relates to the outside world around us, environment also refers to the inside world of the body and its cells. For example, genes can control how a brain is built or how brain cells "talk" with each other. The environment can affect when those genes are "activated" and even change them. Parental age is one factor linked to autism in a child, and it's possible that aging alters genes in the reproductive cells in some way.

Other relevant environmental factors are hard to pin down. Scientists can't experiment on humans to find these factors because to do so would, of course, be unethical. The role of factors like air pollution thus must be sorted out in messy studies that can only imply an association. For air pollution, for example, researchers might compare U.S. zip codes, autism diagnoses in those zip code areas, and the proximity of the areas to power plants to see whether autism rates fluctuate with distance from the plants.

There are hints that a severe infection during pregnancy might contribute to autism. Such an infection might influence brain development through an immune response or through the virus itself.

Co-occurring Conditions

This book takes a deeper look at co-occurring conditions in two separate chapters. Here, I want to mention that these conditions can be psychological, neurodevelopmental (concerning the development of the brain), or medical/physical. Some common conditions that coexist with autism include anxiety, depression, intellectual disability, sleep disorders, connective tissue disorders, epilepsy, and gastrointestinal conditions.

These co-occurring conditions, or *comorbidities*, can impact quality of life for those with autism and the state of their health. If there are autism-related communication barriers, for instance, an autistic person may struggle to describe their symptoms or to get appropriate medical care. In addition, these other conditions might eat up the lion's share of attention, draining resources away from supports related to autism.

Gender Identity

Gender identity also gets a closer look in later chapters, but it is important to mention in this overview because of the considerable overlap between having autism and being gender diverse (Kallitsounaki & Williams, 2023), or not identifying with the sex one was assigned at birth. A 2020 study of more than 600,000 people found that gender-diverse people—those who are transgender, nonbinary, or gender-queer—are up to six times more likely to be autistic than people who identify with the sex they were assigned at birth (Warrier et al., 2020). The reverse, as intuition might suggest, is also the case: Autistic people are more likely than neurotypical people to be gender diverse.

The same study also linked higher rates of depression and autism with being gender diverse. Given that adolescence is the time that gender expression comes into full bloom, these associations are especially important to understand and consider when parenting an autistic teenager.

Other Considerations

In this book, I am mindful about language. The long-time assumption around disability has been that we should use "person-first" language—that is, place the person before the disability. A person's neurobiological status has emerged as a specific case, however. For many autistic self-advocates, person-first language—*person with autism*—separates them in an unwanted way from their identity as autistic people. For this reason, I use *autistic person* preferentially throughout this book.

This book is neurodiversity positive. The concept of neurodiversity often has been misunderstood and misrepresented. The term simply captures the wide range of human behavior: the diversity of "neurotypes" (types of brains, essentially) present within our species. Some neurotypes may not be common or considered typical. A positive view of neurodiversity is that this spectrum of common and rare neurotypes also presents as a spectrum of strengths and deficits. When working with an autistic teenager, it is important to embrace their strengths and not just pay attention to their struggles. An understanding of these strengths will support the pursuit of a thriving, self-determined, good-quality adult life.

In addition, nonautistic people often are referred to as *neurotypical* in comparison to autistic people. The word neurotypical in this context, however, assumes that nonautistic people don't have other human developmental or mental health conditions. Yet most people have "their something." For this reason, I often will use *nonautistic* instead.

The autism *spectrum* itself captures a highly diverse group of people who, in addition to having autism, express a rainbow of human behaviors. For this reason, not every section of this book will be relevant for the autistic teen in your life or to everyone on the spectrum. I have strived to include different examples, cases, and information to represent this great diversity.

Chapter Two

The Secondary School Years

The transition from elementary school to the wider world of middle school and high school can be rough for everyone. Few people seem to look back on middle school, for example, with anything better than mixed positive and negative feelings. These are not usually easy times.

One reason things get harder is that the academics can become more challenging. At the same time, the social environment almost certainly will be trickier to navigate. An autistic teen may enter this situation needing academic support while feeling and showing differences in social behaviors, understanding, and interactions. They may struggle more than ever as a result. That said, autistic teens sometimes don't share the stereotypical teenage obsession with appearances, which could offer protection against some of the common social trials and tribulations of adolescence. Not every autistic adolescent has specific problems during this period.

As these years progress, like many young people, autistic teens can gain skills and understanding and flourish. What will be crucial is how well adults and peers understand, appreciate, and react to the autistic student's strengths and support needs.

Juggling harder schoolwork and complicated social behaviors at the same time can prove overwhelming for autistic people. Compared with nonautistic people, they may need to work their brains much harder during social interactions. If their mental energy is sapped for social survival, it may not be available for academic success. Balancing social and academic needs requires special attention during these years and likely some committed adult support. Tony's experience illustrates the tension.

Tony

I struggled through most of high school, primarily as a result of depression and confusing expectations regarding my academics through an IEP [Individualized Education Program]. My accommodations were inconsistent, not in terms of how they were applied, but in terms of logic and goals. No goals were stated, in fact.

I had two teachers who made a huge difference. One teacher nominated me for a minor biology award, which was the first time I had ever been positively singled out by a teacher or received an award. Another was my Spanish teacher, who I had roundly abused. And yet, she treated me with the most grace, and when I had to be out of school for a few weeks, she sent me a card with a long message of support, which I still have.

I eventually went to a different type of learning environment for my final year, which was self-paced and self-directed, because I wasn't on track to graduate on time. The ability to focus on just one class at a time instead of eight during the day was huge. I remember finishing economics and my final year of history in two weeks each. I ended up graduating several months early.

Once Tony found himself in an environment focused entirely on his schoolwork, he was able to excel on that front. Many nonautistic people can relate to the difficulty of keeping track of eight classes a day. After expending mental resources on making it through the planning and social aspects of such a packed schedule, it's no wonder that an autistic person might have very little left for schoolwork.

Shifting Trajectories

The years covering middle school and high school are a time of considerable change for almost any child, including autistic children. What that change looks like for autistic teens may be unique to them. Their thinking abilities can fluctuate, as can how intense their disability is, with some days being more manageable than others. They can also have learning trajectories that shift unpredictably (Fountain et al., 2012). As with all students, environmental factors, including socioeconomic status and parental education level, can affect how things go during these years (Fountain et al., 2012).

Some researchers have sought to categorize these changes for autistic people. Studies suggest, for example, that about a tenth of autistic children might shift from being "severely affected" to being "high functioning" later in life (Fountain et al., 2012).

I try to avoid the use of functioning labels because they almost always reference the intelligence quotient, or IQ, and other measures of cognition (the mental process of thinking and learning), rather than outward functioning, as it pertains specifically to having autism. But IQ scores, for better or for worse, are often used to categorize autistic children and guide their educational plan. IQ scores are believed to reflect something unchangeable, like eye color or attached earlobes. But that's not the case in general. Studies indicate that for adolescents—including autistic people—these scores can sometimes change during childhood development.

Decisions about placements in school may rely, at least in part, on IQ testing. Research suggests, however, that IQ might not be especially stable, especially in autistic children. A 2022 study of 119 autistic children followed their IQ trajectories for 20 years (Prigge et al., 2022). Their scores were lower than those of nonautistic children at a young age but increased faster with age than in nonautistic people. Into early adulthood, scores for specific parts of IQ tests can continue to fluctuate. For autistic children, later scores can differ substantially from earlier childhood scores. Nevertheless, an IQ score offers a snapshot in time for guiding resource and support choices, even if it might change at an older age.

The authors of the 2022 study concluded that because IQ can change, a single test can't capture the intellectual ability of an autistic child. Instead, looking at scores on tests repeated over time might be more informative (Prigge et al., 2022). Other studies have found an increase in IQ through later childhood and into adolescence in autistic people. One group of researchers reported an average rise of 7.5 IQ points from ages 12 to 23 years (Simonoff et al., 2020).

Scores for IQ tests can be presented as percentiles, which indicates a relative performance on the test. For example, a score in the 98th percentile indicates a performance that is as good as or better than that of 98% of the people taking the test.

The *full-scale* score, which is what most people mean when they talk about a person's IQ, is the intelligence quotient itself. It is calculated based on the test scores of a specific population at a specific age. Someone who has an IQ of 100 has a dead-center average IQ score. An increase of 7.5 points would mean an increase from 100 to 107.5, still within the range of average intelligence. Most people who take these tests fall within a score range of 85 to 115.

Even with increases in IQ scores, however, other traits that are specific to autism may not follow a similar trajectory. One 4-year study of autistic children found that how they interacted socially remained relatively stable during the study period. From age 13 to their late teens, fewer than a fifth of the children showed any tendency to interact in a different, potentially more neurotypical way (Scheeren et al., 2020). The authors concluded that, unlike their IQ, how autistic teens interact socially may not change much over time.

Take the example of Lucas. His cognitive (thinking and learning) testing scores in elementary school showed a pattern that is not uncommon for autistic children: average to high scores on some parts of the test and quite low, single-digit percentile scores on others. Lucas also had learning delays, especially in reading. Yet in high school, his performance did not suggest intellectual disability, and he scored more consistently within the high-average range across the test. His reading specialist reported that Lucas seemed to have "learned to read overnight." Lucas took honors classes, including in math, his specific interest. His cognitive testing scores had changed, yes, but Lucas still manifested the core features of having autism, especially in his social interactions and interests.

For autistic people, cognitive testing scores within the "normal" range do not seem to protect them against negative experiences related to autistic traits, such as social understanding and emotional regulation. Regardless of IQ, autistic students in the teen years and beyond still need autism-specific support and understanding to maximize their independence.

The support that autistic students need as they enter the teen years varies and changes with time. As you'll see later in the chapter, this expectation of change is reflected in the re-evaluation of need every 3 years for school accommodations planning. An autistic student may have had accommodations in their younger years that need to be updated and adjusted during adolescence. Parents may notice that access to service-based sources falters as their child ages or that something that once worked no longer does. Parents should be alert to intensifying struggles and look for ways to build "sensory breaks" into the day. These breaks from the hustle and bustle of classrooms, hallways, and cafeterias can reduce mental demands on autistic kids and offer them downtime for regrouping and recovery. Growing up is an ongoing process, with numerous fluctuations and changing trajectories, and accommodations and adjustments should follow suit.

In this book, these needs are discussed in terms of level of support, that is, high, low, and medium. Students with high-support needs might benefit from the most intensive support on several fronts. Students needing low support may require only minor accommodations in class to function well.

It's useful to remember that environment can be a strong factor in the level of support needs. For example, a quiet environment or quiet places for breaks might well reduce a child's level of need from medium support to low support. Autistic people have told me that a quiet room or retreat from the social demands of middle school and high school was crucial for surviving the day. Taking a break from the emotionally heightened, complex world of adolescent interactions at school gave them the respite they needed to manage both academic and social demands.

Mixing or Separating Social and Academic Demands

One factor I've observed in my experiences with autistic young people is that mixing academic and social demands at the same time can be overwhelming. For any teen, social demands can completely overshadow academic pursuits. That's part of this life stage: learning lessons about human interactions, behavior, and time management. In this way, young people build out a toolkit for adulthood. But think about Tony, described previously, who finished school on his own. An autistic student may find it extremely difficult to juggle social and scholastic demands at once during their school time and may benefit from clear boundaries between them.

One mother of a now-adult autistic son told me that when her son was about to enter kindergarten, she decided to keep him out of school for 2 more years. Her reasoning was that his developmental stage lagged about a year behind that of his average peers but was always trending upward and progressing. She says that this decision, based on what she knew about her son and not on standardized expectations around age or school, was "the best decision I ever made with him. I will never, ever regret it."

The space those years afforded gave her son "time to build confidence in who he was," she says. She knew he'd probably be OK academically. But she wanted him to deal with the social piece more slowly, holding off on dropping him into a social setting until he could mature a little more.

> ### Sidebar: Autism-Specific Schools and Homeschool
>
> Some families consider moving away from a conventional school environment, whether public or private, in favor of schools designed specifically for autistic students or homeschooling. As Tony described, in their experience, moving to a "self-directed" and "self-paced" learning environment was the right path for them. But research also indicates that a conventional, mainstream school environment may offer greater benefit for some autistic students, possibly because of more interaction with a diversity of peers (McGuire & Veenstra-VanderWeele, 2020). Regardless of what families and autistic students favor, the important outcome is a balance between academic accommodation and access to important social experiences with peers. In my experience, homeschooling families can gain access to these social interactions through participation in homeschool collaboratives or pods, outings organized by local homeschool groups, and other social settings such as sports, clubs, or religious-based or other youth groups.

Types of Classroom Support

In high school, classroom directions can become longer and more complex. Social interactions become more subtle and nuanced. The schools themselves are usually much larger. In other words, everything multiplies. These factors can be overwhelming, even for nonautistic newcomers. For people who need time and space and straightforward communication, the change can feel like a tsunami.

Autistic teens may find it hard to communicate with nonautistic people and come to a mutually satisfactory understanding. Social interactions can be broken down roughly into three steps:

- understanding what's being communicated to you (in writing, spoken word, or nonverbal cues, also known as receptive language);
- communicating clearly to someone else (known as expressive language or communication); and
- interactions with others that involve both understanding and expression.

Important factors in these steps include how rapidly an autistic person can process or produce language and other forms of communication.

Autistic people may take a beat to catch up with, say, a list of spoken instructions. During that pause to catch up, they might miss more steps that are being explained. In the classroom, at home, and in social situations, autistic people may need more time or incremental delivery of information. They also need others to make an effort to understand their forms of communication. The *interaction* part of communication means that both parties do some work in understanding each other, without the entire burden being placed on the autistic person.

Classroom adjustments are possible and can be a lifeline amid the flood of newness and noise of high school. Parents or the autistic student can discuss with school faculty and teachers how to recognize and adapt to the teen's specific communication needs. Following are some examples of what that might look like (based on Butler & Dykstra, 2014):

Imran

When passing out a quiz, Mr. Lee asks the class to turn over the quiz when they've finished it, take out their class notebooks, open the textbook to page 200, and start taking notes on the reading. Imran completes his test and then takes out his textbook, without turning the test over or getting his class notebook. To Mr. Lee, this looks like an attempt to cheat. But in reality, Imran didn't process the two middle steps of the instructions. A solution would be for Mr. Lee to write out multistep lists like this one on the board, keeping the verbal instruction simple, such as "Look at the board for instructions once you've finished the quiz," and place his hand on the board next to the written list, as a visual emphasis.

Morgan

Morgan needs to step out for a drink of water because she is thirsty. She says to her teacher, Ms. Anders, "Do you need a drink?" Swapping pronouns can be a feature of autistic communication. Alert listeners can work to detect when an expression with "you" really reflects a reference to "I" and respond accordingly.

Enrique

Enrique's parents know that when they talk to him, they need to wait a few moments for him to process and show that he's heard them. Unaware adults tend to interpret the delay from Enrique as oppositional, and it may seem like he's ignoring them. To avoid this miscommunication with the adults who are teaching and working with Enrique, his parents explain the situation and their strategy for giving him time to process their words and respond. In this way, they ensure that Enrique's behavior is not misunderstood, preventing the stress and bad feelings that could escalate.

Generating speech in the moment can be a big lift for autistic people. Some will adopt words, phrases, or sounds they have heard or read that hold specific meaning for them and use them instead. The practice of repeating a heard phrase over and over is called *echolalia*, although people may also repeat phrases that they have read rather than heard. These phrases have been described in some definitions as "meaningless." Autistic people, however, report that they use echolalia purposefully. It's a comfortable and familiar way to express a feeling or need when accessing words becomes too hard.

Especially in stressful or unfamiliar situations, relying on these familiar and useful phrases can be an antidote to anxiety. Echoing also serves other purposes, such as self-managing emotional responses, or for *stimming*, a release following a strong surge of feeling. But echolalia is open to all kinds of interpretation. If the echo follows directly after something someone has just said, its meaning may differ from a phrase frequently used to communicate need, feeling, or opinion.

For example, if someone asks Jony, "Do you want some M&Ms?," Jony might say, "Want some M&Ms." There are different possible interpretations of this echolalia. Jony might be agreeing that they want M&Ms. But they also could just be confirming that that is what was being asked. Tone is not necessarily an indicator because autistic people may use language tone and pacing that nonautistic people don't use or expect. The key is to learn the lexicon of the autistic person—the terms and phrases they use to indicate specific thoughts and feelings—and to interpret their language, just as we might do for anyone else (think of trying to understand current slang among adolescents).

As social interactions become more subtle and sometimes feel scary, an autistic person's communication strategies and their communication disabilities may complicate things even more. The social aspects of being an autistic adolescent, including perspective taking and empathy, are covered in more detail in Chapter five. Briefly, some groups recommend that educators and support staff use techniques of *social engineering*—forming friend groups or lunch bunches, for example—as ways of supporting autistic students. The potential pitfalls and benefits of this are also discussed in Chapter five.

Sidebar: Alternative and Augmentative Communication

As noted in the "twins" story in Chapter one, tools referred to as *augmentative and alternative communication* are available to autistic individuals and their families (and with varying amounts of evidence of effectiveness). Often, the tools are digital devices that generate speech or applications that can be used on smartphones or tablets. They can also be nondigital, like a set of ready-made pictures depicting common classroom activities that can be used to create a daily schedule.

If an autistic person has already been in a classroom for a few years, these types of tools likely have been used or suggested. As schedules or material become more complex—secondary education often involves a different teacher and classroom for each subject—these tools may become even more important, along with coordinating their use (Butler & Dykstra, 2014).

Wish List: Strategies for Success

The previously discussed information describes some changes and adaptations that can be made in the classroom for autistic people. But more strategies are available for teachers and support staff to use—and parents and autistic students can suggest them.

To generate a wish list of potential methods of support, I asked autistic adults to look back on their own experiences in secondary school and recall what they found most supportive and positive. Much of what they said would be appropriate for any student who finds themselves struggling academically and socially:

- *Predictable space during unpredictable times of day.* The unstructured times during the school day can be the hardest for autistic students. They often have to expend greater than average energy navigating social situations while needing downtime to regroup during a busy, often confusing day. Predictable spaces include quiet rooms, the library, and classrooms where teachers allow a few students to spend quiet time during unstructured periods. One respondent said they would have preferred to spend recess on their own, "in silence," but there was no space for them to do so.
- *Trusted adults.* Having at least one or two adults whom they trust, or who "get it," was a common theme. Some mentioned teachers who went to the mat for them to ensure their inclusion in general education classrooms. Having someone they trusted who could help them interpret "hidden social rules" was also important. These trusted adults may form a part of the *transition support team*, an important element of the transition out of high school for autistic people, as discussed in the last chapter of this book.
- *Routine.* Disruptions in routines, for example, for big assemblies or half days, can create particular times of stress. If they know how such disruptions can affect autistic students—and probably nonautistic students as well, for that matter—teachers and staff can prepare their students ahead of time, using the communication tools that work best for the students.

- *Concrete instructions.* Open-ended assignments, such as having to pluck a research topic from thin air rather than from a provided list, is one example of the frustration autistic people expressed about needing concrete guidance. Taking big projects one piece at a time, with clear instructions regarding what to turn in for each piece, was also cited as helpful.

My respondents cited a sense of struggle with factors that introduced chaos into the day, made them late for class, or caused confusion. Common challenges included a large campus with far-flung classrooms and lockers far away from it all. Mandatory gym classes that required sports participation and changing in a locker room were cited as especially negative experiences. As one autistic adult commented, "Gym class was absolute hell."

For autistic students, other accommodations can mean plans for addressing distressed behaviors and anxiety, including anticipating and preventing triggers in certain situations. Here's an example: A teacher has a practice of randomly assigning students their seat in class as they enter the room, handing each student a seat number that corresponds to a number on a desk. The teacher's intent is to mix up students for work in small groups and to keep students from always sitting with friends (and distracting one another). But Elijah, an autistic student in the class, finds the prospect of sitting in an unpredictable place every day extremely stressful and anxiety inducing. The teacher agrees to give Elijah his seat number as he leaves class each day so that he knows exactly where he will be sitting the next time the class meets.

Generalized Coping Strategies

Tools that are effective in different environments (like home and school) can support routine and keep an autistic teen's life more predictable. Being at school all day doesn't mean your teen will inevitably fall apart the minute they get home—they can use their schedulers, communication tools, and coping techniques across environments (Aitken & Fletcher-Watson, 2022). Reducing the buildup of stress in any given context leaves mental energy available for learning elsewhere, so across settings (home, sports, school), the goal is to set up a predictable, achievable daily routine for your student (Aitken & Fletcher-Watson, 2022). Giving concrete instructions with clear expectations can translate across daily environments and support the sense of structure and routine.

Sensory overload is a key part of the autistic experience. As noted earlier, one important strategy for success is to give students the space they need for low-sensory time during the day. Autistic students should have options away from bright lights, crowded noisy rooms, and free-for-all time if they need a sensory break. Chaotic times like dressing for or participating in gym class and the lunch period will probably need special attention because they can be triggers for anxiety and distressed behaviors. Having quiet spaces to regroup can support emotional regulation—the ability to recognize and identify an emotion, accept it, and take the steps needed to manage it. This regulation can, in turn, support a sense of calmness and successful navigation of the school day, with effects that can last into the evening at home.

> ### Sidebar: Universal Design
>
> The concept of *universal design* is that accommodations for disabled people are also useful for people without the disability. Examples in the classroom include tablets and laptops that have practical tools or a visual schedule made available for the entire class, not just for autistic students (Aitken & Fletcher-Watson, 2022). Research suggests that with adjustments that have potential benefits beyond the target population, many other student populations may benefit as well (Friskney et al., 2019). For parents and students who struggle to have accommodation needs met, highlighting these extended benefits may be useful.

> ### Sidebar: Other Tips for School
>
> Other tips for navigating school include the following (Rentschler et al., 2022):
> - Find clubs or hobbies that might interest the student and match their passions, or even start a new club related to an important interest.
> - In keeping with what autistic adults told us, identify one or more "champions" on the campus who can be eyes, ears, mentors, and advocates, if needed.
> - Educate the campus population about neurodiversity, including autism, and how all people both differ from one another and share similarities; talk about how communication might look between people with different neurotypes.

Know the System

If you're the parent of an autistic student who was identified at an early age and is receiving supports through (public) elementary school, you're probably familiar with "the system."

An important part of parenting a child through the secondary school years is to set aside fears and be bold as an advocate, because you can't do these years over again. Federal law requires that all children be able to access a free and appropriate education in the least restrictive environment possible. That means that attending school with peers is the overall aim to meet the standard of "least restrictive environment," within which the education should be appropriate.

Parents can seek to develop connections with teachers and staff who can be advocates on the ground for the student. These connections are important because regardless of a child's autism status, the "village" part of childrearing comes to the fore during adolescence. Children are no longer within their parents' sights at all times (which is developmentally appropriate) and are learning to navigate the world for themselves. The hope is that they are provided with the best tools to do so. A good relationship with teachers and staff can make the difference between Individualized Education Program (IEP) meetings that end with a useful and effective road map and those that lead to litigation (Bolourian et al., 2019).

What if teachers and staff seem unaware of or resistant to what's needed for an effective IEP that everyone honors? Consider asking the administration about holding a training session that brings faculty and staff up to date on what the law and good teaching practices require. At the end of this book, I have included a link to one such training offering with the Center on Secondary Education for Students With Autism Spectrum Disorder.

If things reach a point of immoveable disagreement, families can turn to family advocates to support them. These advocates work within the system to establish an education plan that meets federal requirements and is in the best interest of the autistic child. The Wrightslaw website (see Resources, Chapter 2) has useful information about special education advocates, their role, what parents can do before reaching that point, and how to be a child's best advocate in IEP meetings. Adolescents who want to serve as their own advocates or work with other adults can also find tips and information at the site.

Even with these steps in place, in a big school system where teachers and staff are stretched thin and education budgets are dwindling, students may fall through the cracks. There are strategies parents can pursue to make sure their student stays on solid ground, especially if they are self-advocating in their IEP meetings. These include:

- identifying peers who are willing to be supportive of the student in transitioning to a new setting—such as a new school, new classes, or new team;
- looking over the meeting agenda before a meeting and noting areas of concern;
- conducting meetings in a predictable, routine way each time, with limited changes, except those needed for accessibility reasons;
- making sure everyone at the meeting introduces themselves and describes their role; and
- being familiar with the rights of students with disabilities and what the law requires.

Finally, always keep records of everything. It's a good idea to start and maintain a binder or binders for all records on your child's education. When the time arrives for transition planning—which ideally is when your child enters high school—you'll be glad you kept these records.

The Individuals With Disabilities Education Act, Part B, and Special Education Services: 504 Versus IEP and Planning for College

What goes into the planning for supports will depend on the identified needs of the autistic student. As many parents and autistic students will know by the time secondary school rolls around, the key piece of the IEP is which accommodations it includes. Accommodations are the adjustments and environmental changes that can be made at school—in the classroom, in unstructured times, in teaching approaches—that give the student the ability to learn successfully.

How accommodations look varies considerably from person to person and school to school. There are some standard tactics. One is motor breaks—incorporated carefully to avoid attracting notice and potentially stigma. For example, a student might be asked to deliver something to the office at the midway point of class each day. Or all students might have a motor break together because, quite often, an accommodation intended to help a neurodivergent student ends up being useful for all students. Overall, the goal is to provide tools so that students can learn at the same pace as their peers, gain skills they need to progress, and maintain their privacy.

One kind of plan for using these strategies is the 504 plan. This was put into place as Section 504 of the Rehabilitation Act of 1973. This law states that a child whose disability interferes with their ability to learn and be successful in the classroom can be evaluated and have a 504 plan developed for them. The meetings for a 504 plan don't necessarily involve parents by law, so parents who want to be present will need to request attendance.

At a minimum, the plan should list the academic strategies that will be used and who will make sure they're implemented. If things aren't going as you and your autistic child would like, negotiating with the school is a first step in remedying the problem. If that's unsuccessful, other options are available. This law is an antidiscrimination law, so families with students in publicly funded schools that don't seem to be following the law can file a discrimination complaint with the U.S. Department of Education's Office for Civil Rights.

The 504 plan is a looser and less bureaucratically safeguarded plan than an IEP for providing accommodations for students. As the Wrightslaw website explains, it ensures equal access to education. But the 504 does not require an IEP, which lays out more specific, unique accommodations to ensure educational benefit for the student. The primary use of a 504 plan is for students who need a few tweaks in a general-population classroom, such as motor breaks or extra time on tests, to keep them on pace with their peers (https://www.wrightslaw.com/info/sec504.index.htm). The IEP comes in when a student needs specific services during the school day to ensure access to education and tailored accommodations.

The basis for the IEP is a different federal law, the Individuals With Disabilities Education Act, known as IDEA in IEP circles. This law was reauthorized as the Individuals With Disabilities Education Improvement Act in 2004 and updated in 2017 to include considerations of race and ethnicity. It is much stricter in its requirements on all sides than the 504 statute.

To qualify for an IEP, students must undergo an evaluation that establishes the presence of a qualifying disability that negatively impacts their educational performance. These evaluations may include educational psychology assessments, occupational therapy and speech–language pathologist assessments, and others. The centerpiece of the law is the least restrictive environment factor: that students receiving supports through an IEP must be educated in the least restrictive environment possible. In most cases, the aim is for the student to spend as much time as possible in the general student population.

The main components of the IEP are the student's current status in school in terms of academic and functional performance (meaning their ability to perform routine tasks throughout the school day), with a description of how the student's disability interferes with the latter. The IEP must include goals for the year that can be tracked and quantified, goals that are ideally described as specific, measurable, attainable, relevant, and time bound (also known as SMART goals).

The IEP must also include information regarding how progress will be measured, along with a description of the evidence-based services the child will receive. Finally, the plan must characterize how least restrictive the child's education will be, that is, how much of it will be in the general-education classroom setting.

It is possible for students to have multiple "labels" for the educational context, such as a dual diagnosis of autism and attention-deficit/hyperactivity disorder, and they may have both a 504 plan and an IEP. Autistic students may also be labeled "gifted" and receive a separate series of related services, depending on what the school offers for students who are given this label.

As you might imagine, sometimes IEP meetings and the process of setting relevant goals can be stressful and tense. But districts are improving in establishing full inclusion policies for students instead of shunting them into "special" classrooms away from the general-education population (Boulorian et al., 2019). That doesn't mean that all parents are happy with full inclusion or that all districts have established such policies. Research suggests that IEP plans for autistic students tend to be the most often contested, although at the same time, the trend for autistic students may be that they are spending more time in general-education classrooms. When autistic students do receive education in a general-education setting, they tend to do better compared with autistic peers who are placed in specialized, segregated classrooms.

The Transition Plan

By the time a student turns 16 (but preferably starting much earlier, at entry into high school), the IEP must also include a transition plan that describes the student's plans after graduation and what supports they will need for a successful transition. Legally, the IEP must include information about assessments needed, goals following graduation, the remaining course of high school study, and services needed to achieve these goals. The final chapter of this book goes into more detail about planning for this transition.

The transition assessment will incorporate what the autistic student and their family share with the IEP team about these aims, along with possible obstacles to achieving these goals. The autistic student's current state of readiness for adult life will also be part of the assessment, including skills in independent living. An interview may help sort out interests after high school and which will be the best choice among the various paths available—for example, college, work, or professional or technical training.

This information should be maintained in a portfolio that is specific to transition, the summary of performance portfolio. This portfolio will contain the goals of the student and the activities the student needs to engage in to reach these goals. These goals are both short term (completed within the year) and long term (a few years out). A short-term goal might be to develop a resume to apply for jobs. A long-term goal might be to get the training needed to become an electrician. The activities to achieve these goals will depend on the goals themselves, but can involve educational activities and activities in the community.

All students who have a transition meeting can request in writing that the school district invite a representative from their state's department of rehabilitation. This department is ultimately responsible for providing some of the transition services that support students' postsecondary goals. The department assesses whether someone is eligible for services before providing them. If they determine that the student is eligible, they will develop an individualized plan for employment before the student leaves school.

This is all overwhelming, and families often find themselves stuck between organizations or departments that seem to want to shuffle responsibility onto each other. For more information about these processes, parents and students can consult the state-based Parent Training and Information Centers, which were established to support families in navigating the tangle of laws, bureaucracy, paperwork, and meetings. The resources list at the end of this book has a link to a search page so you can find a center near you.

For information more oriented to students who self-advocate, the Autistic Self Advocacy Network maintains a page with plain-language summaries and more detailed information about the Americans With Disabilities Act and other laws, along with toolkits and handbooks for autistic students working on their transition to adulthood. Links to these resources are also provided at the end of the book.

Regardless of which kind of plan is in place, it's important to stay on top of things. It's also crucial to keep records of meeting agendas and minutes, emails, grade reports and comments, notes from conferences with teachers, testing results—everything—in the binder(s) you maintain for your child.

> ### Sidebar: Concerns About Abuse at School
>
> Every parent of a disabled child likely has special concerns about whether their child is suffering abuse at school. If communication impairments are part of the disability, those concerns can be heightened.
>
> The following list includes some red flags to watch for. They should trigger a request for attention from administration and other authorities.
>
> - sudden changes in behaviors at home, such as lashing out in unusual ways
> - fearful behavior that is not characteristic of the individual, such as suddenly resisting going to school although they have been OK with it previously
> - behavior changes that reflect anxiety or an onset or increase in nightmares
>
> If you see any of these red flags, start asking questions and maybe even keep your child at home until you get things figured out. If your concerns don't receive the attention you feel they deserve, there are other options. School districts have a uniform code of complaint. Call the district office and they should direct you to the appropriate website for submitting a complaint, which you should direct to the superintendent.
>
> The U.S. Office for Civil Rights also has a portal for filing a discrimination complaint. Parents can contact their elected officials and

> let them know that they've filed a uniform complaint in their district and/or a civil rights complaint and ask to copy them on it.
>
> For students with an Individualized Education Program or 504 plan in place, another option is to use the plan to remove your child from the potentially unsafe situation and into one that you describe as better equipped to provide equitable access to the required learning. This change could be a request for removal to a different classroom or even a different school.

K–12 Strengths-Based Approach

In an education chapter, I would be remiss if I left out best practices in education itself for autistic students. A 2023 panel at Stanford's Neurodiversity Project discussed using a strengths-based approach to education, rather than focusing on the *deficit model* of what's "wrong." As one neurodivergent panelist noted, if children are always hearing that they have something wrong that needs to be fixed, they may internalize the idea that they are broken.

Rather than focusing on wrong deviations from some elusive norm, a strengths-based approach focuses on ways a student can use their strengths to help themselves. Even parents who may have been socialized to watching for and noticing only deficits may have overlooked these strengths.

Previously, I mentioned some ways that autistic students can find engagement and interest in school by joining clubs focused on subjects of great interest to them, which one of the panelists called *monotropism*. Starting with a passion or a real competency in a subject can open the path to building skills in social communication and identifying like-minded peers. After all, that's how nonautistic people go about finding each other. Yet some assessment and accommodation pathways veer away from these monotropisms, identifying them as deficits to fix instead of a strength and a tool for accessing more skills.

Video games offer an example. Adults of pre–video game generations tend to deplore a gameplay habit. But in the early 21st century, the ability to play a video game well can be a strength, including a social strength, and lends itself to all kinds of openings to new skills. Gameplay can be a springboard to being creative (world building), establishing social networks (many games include multiple players and require collaboration among players), and even playing out social scenarios in ways that can apply to real life. As with any activity, it's also important to find where the boundary should be in engagement to leave space for other activities and other aspects of teenage life.

Another example is a child who relies heavily on logic and structure and wants everything to be in a certain order or a certain way. Leaning into that strength as a way to organize their day or schoolwork emphasizes an appreciation and respect for their way of being and shows how they can use it to support other skills. They can apply their interest, for example, to understand the structure of an argument essay and why it is organized a certain way.

Knowing where a child is strongest offers a path to learning. A child often benefits from knowing a "why" before they're asked to "do." Autistic children especially may benefit from having this gap bridged for them. Instead of simply saying, "Read pages 10 to 15 in your textbook," an educator can offer context: "We are going to read pages 10 to 15 in our textbook because we will learn four new things and revisit four pieces of information we already know, which will help us remember them better."

Another key piece of advice is to let autistic people be themselves rather than trying to mask who they are. Autistic advocates say that the effort to mask or "camouflage" themselves as not having autism is exhausting. It may lead to decent "performances" at school but end in a complete loss of control at home because of drained mental resources and built-up anxiety. Parents can even emphasize how they overlap in some traits with their child in positive ways, creating a culture of inclusion that makes a child feel accepted and loved for who they are.

Chapter Three

Autism and Co-occurring Genetic and Medical Conditions

Autism often overlaps with other conditions, including epilepsy, intellectual disability, joint hypermobility, genetic disorders such as fragile X syndrome, and mood and anxiety disorders (the next chapter addresses mental health in detail; Glans et al., 2022). Studies have suggested that about 1 in 4 autistic people have a significant medical condition. Almost 1 in 10 have co-occurring epilepsy. Intellectual disability together with autism seems to increase the risk for other medical conditions by as much as nine times compared with autism alone. Large studies in Denmark, Taiwan, Australia, and Finland have shown more eye, facial, and other developmental anomalies among autistic children, more so for autistic people with intellectual disability (Clothier & Absoud, 2021).

Here, you'll find information about some of the genetic conditions that overlap with autism and medical issues that are more common among autistic people (as mentioned, I address psychological conditions in the next chapter). For each of these co-occurring conditions, I provide a brief overview of signs and symptoms and how each arises, the interaction with autism, and the role of adolescence. Although I sometimes describe treatments and therapies, you should talk with your family's medical care providers about any concerns or questions.

Having autism can mean increased risk for other conditions for several reasons. Nonspeaking autistic people, for example, may find it difficult to let others know about any symptoms they might be experiencing, which can delay diagnosis and treatment. When they are properly armed with information, autistic people and their families and clinicians can be on the lookout for clues to common, co-occurring conditions and take steps to address them. Many of these issues don't become evident until puberty or become more or less important in the adolescent years. For this reason, the teenage years can be a turning point for an autistic person's mental and medical healthcare needs.

Before getting to the overviews of some of these conditions, I think it's important to address a few key related themes. First, there are many claims about what various treatments, therapies, supplements, and so on can do. Trying to sort out their true value or expected effectiveness for autism or a co-occurring condition can be overwhelming. I have developed and included a checklist (see the section "Sifting Evidence") to help you sift through these claims.

The second important theme is what's known as *diagnostic overshadowing*. In this situation, a condition is overlooked because its signs or symptoms are chalked up to another known diagnosis. Autism itself can overshadow other conditions in this way, or another condition can interfere with recognizing the features of autism.

The third important factor is the role of sex (and gender). Sex (and gender) can influence how someone expresses their autism. It also can affect conditions that commonly occur with autism, their frequency, and whether they are detected. One straightforward example is fragile X syndrome, which tends to affect people who bear a Y chromosome (people assigned male at birth). As a more subtle example, complaints of pain are more likely to be overlooked or dismissed if the person experiencing the pain identifies as female (Earp et al., 2019). This is especially important given the higher rate of painful connective tissue disorders among autistic people. Both fragile X and connective tissue disorders are discussed in more detail later in this chapter.

Sifting Evidence

When you or a loved one experiences a health or other condition that is complicated to diagnose or lacks established treatment, it's tempting to try what are known as *off-label recommendations*. These are treatments or therapies that are established for one condition, but commonly used for another. Many of these recommendations are for supplements and other products that claim to offer symptom relief. I am not going to get into the value of specific interventions, supplements, or other possible therapies or dismiss out of hand everything you might encounter. But I would like to offer the following checklist of precautions to consider before you try something that isn't approved by the U.S. Food and Drug Administration or that lacks evidence of effectiveness based on clinical studies. Note that these suggestions are broadly applicable when considering whether to invest time and resources into a given treatment; they are not specific to co-occurring medical or genetic conditions.

1. Check the source of the recommendation and their expertise in the medical specialty related to the claim. Not all expertise comes from a classroom, but training in a specialty such as medicine for many years does make a difference in a person's understanding and experience.
2. Consider the agenda of the person or group presenting the information. If it's a scientific paper, look at the funders (who paid for the research). A conflict of interest isn't always a problem, but it does warrant adding a grain of salt to your considerations. And ask yourself whether someone is telling you about a problem you never even knew existed and then offering to sell you a "solution" to it.
3. Consider the language being used to support a claim, especially if it promises a cure. Sometimes a string of scientific words sounds compelling and authentic but is total nonsense. Consult someone with training in chemistry or biology if you think claims sound suspicious or unlikely.
4. Examine the kind of evidence offered in support of a treatment—not only who funded it but also what *kind* of evidence it is. Is it testimonials or product reviews, rather than well-planned and published clinical trials or studies testing a scientific hypothesis? It's easy to create testimonials, and the product review mill that produces fake reviews is notorious.
5. Be wary of claims about exclusivity or proprietary/secret processes or ingredients. It's rare for anything completely new to just emerge on the therapeutic scene. Most treatment interventions and therapies grow from existing knowledge and tools.

6. Be wary of antiestablishmentarian claims, such as, "Your doctor doesn't want you to know." Doctors generally would very much like patients to know about things that will help them feel better.
7. Watch out for "cure-alls." Products touted to help with many unrelated conditions affecting many body systems should draw skepticism.
8. Follow the money or the "sunk costs"—an individual or group's investment in a product. Although money is a strong motivator for people hoping to sell a supplement or therapy, the emotional investment also can be a factor. Someone who has spent much of their own time and energy committed to backing a specific supplement's effects, for example, can be very motivated to stick to their claims, even if they've seen evidence that counters them. Just do a bias check before buying.

Sidebar: Diagnostic Overshadowing

It is important for parents and other caregivers to know that an autism diagnosis can overshadow sometimes life-threatening conditions. Autistic adults have expressed frustration over this problem, as one individual reports: "Once an autism diagnosis is given there is such a reluctance to name anything else because everything (physical and psychological it seems) becomes autism." The reverse, a case of missed autism diagnosis, is also possible: "Because of another disorder like depression or bipolar . . . everything becomes that instead of autism, thus preventing needed diagnosis."

With diagnostic overshadowing, a diagnosis of one condition leads to attributing every sign and symptom to that condition, even if some other problem might be present. For autistic people, the shadow can work in either direction: The autism diagnosis can divert attention from red flags for another condition or disease, or diagnosis with a behavioral condition that overlaps enough with autism can leave the autism unrecognized (Rosen et al., 2018). How can this happen? Some factors include communication impairments, emotional dysregulation, and overlap between features of autism and some other conditions, especially if they are related to behavior or mental health.

For example, autistic people commonly experience sleep difficulties. For this reason, any episode of sleep struggles may be chalked up to autism when, in reality, there might be some other cause, such as gastroesophageal reflux (heartburn). A nonspeaking autistic person may struggle to communicate what their gastrointestinal symptoms are. As a result, their nighttime distress could be attributed to autism-related sleep disruption—with no straightforward treatment—instead of to a highly treatable issue. They end up going untreated and continue to experience the distress.

On the flip side, because autism often involves motor hyperactivity (overactive physical behaviors), someone who also has attention-deficit/hyperactivity disorder (ADHD) might not get the ADHD diagnosis they need. Although there is some overlap between the two (discussed in the next chapter), they have distinct treatment approaches, and effective therapies are especially available for ADHD. Without recognition of the ADHD, however, these effective therapies go unused and the ADHD-related disability the autistic person experiences goes untreated. Other conditions that can be concealed by an autism diagnosis include anxiety, mood disorders like depression and bipolar disorder, eating disorders, and schizophrenia (Rosen et al., 2018; Salem & Kennedy, 2021).

During the adolescent years, many conditions, whether medical or neurobehavioral, can kick up a gear, or their symptoms may start to appear for the first time. Sometimes, even autism itself is not diagnosed until this time. The social deficits of autism don't always become sufficiently obvious until an autistic person has to navigate the complex social seas of middle school and high school. People with diagnosed autism and their parents should pay attention to new or intensified features and rely on autism-literate clinicians for accurate assessments.

If your child hasn't been diagnosed with autism but you believe a diagnosis might be appropriate, it's important for clinicians to have a full history of your child's development, behaviors across different settings (school, home), and any past diagnostic testing. They can examine this information for clues that might have been overlooked (Salem & Kennedy, 2021). As noted in the previous chapter, it's a good idea for families to maintain a binder with all information related to medical and mental health needs, school, work, and other aspects of their child's life. It's also a good idea to encourage young people, autistic or not, to practice appropriate engagement with their medical providers, including going through their medical history with a clinician and asking questions about anything they don't understand. This practice can support young people in taking responsibility for their own care.

Other factors that can overshadow an accurate diagnosis are societal in nature. Gaps in access to healthcare based on race and ethnicity can leave some children without a history of thorough diagnostic testing or overlooked for a specific diagnosis because of a healthcare provider's biases and assumptions. Studies indicate that non-White autistic adults, for example, are less likely than their White counterparts to receive an accurate diagnosis of some psychiatric and medical conditions (Ames et al., 2022). The bottom line is to be wary of automatically chalking up new symptoms to an existing diagnosis.

Sidebar: Sex-Based Differences

Autistic girls and boys may have different odds of co-occurring conditions, with girls tending to have a higher likelihood for many of them. Female sex is linked to higher epilepsy risk in the autistic population

(Bishop et al., 2021). For many reasons, girls represent a smaller proportion of the autistic population than boys, although that proportion has grown along with the recognition that autism can look different between boys and girls.

Among those with an autism diagnosis, however, girls are more likely to have a co-occurring condition. The results of a large 2021 U.S. study of 83,500 children found that autistic girls have higher odds than autistic boys of having most co-occurring conditions (Angell et al., 2021). The authors compared risks between autistic boys and autistic girls at an average age of 8 years. The most common co-occurring conditions were developmental disorders, attention-deficit/hyperactivity disorder (ADHD), and gastrointestinal (GI) disorders. Overall, GI disorders, sleep disorders, and developmental disorders were less likely to be diagnosed with increasing age.

Odds for most co-occurring conditions increase with age, however. These conditions include anxiety disorders like obsessive-compulsive disorder, epilepsy, mood disorders, intellectual disability, GI disorders, and metabolic disorders such as low thyroid and diabetes. Autistic girls are more likely than autistic boys to have any of these, along with sleep disorders, but less likely than boys to have co-occurring ADHD.

These differences matter for several reasons. One is the risk of underdiagnosis of autism in girls because of diagnostic overshadowing from these other conditions. Clinicians may end up focusing on the other condition instead of considering autism. Indeed, girls are also less likely in general than are boys to be diagnosed with ADHD, possibly because of different signs and symptoms of ADHD in girls. Another reason that these differences are important is that some are treatable. An awareness of their greater likelihood in girls could lead to interventions that might support improved quality of life.

Many anatomical and other medical conditions commonly co-occur with autism. Some are part of known genetic syndromes and others are a stand-alone diagnosis. Among the genetic syndromes are *tuberous sclerosis complex* and *fragile X syndrome*, as well as an array of connective tissue–related conditions such as *Ehlers–Danlos syndrome*. Gastrointestinal (GI) difficulties and diagnoses are extremely common among autistic people, along with kidney and urological conditions. Finally, as I noted at the beginning of this chapter, epilepsy is present in about 1 in 10 autistic people.

Co-occurring Genetic Conditions

Tuberous Sclerosis Complex and Fragile X Syndrome

Two genetic anomalies are associated with tuberous sclerosis complex (TSC). It can be inherited by transmission of this genetic material from one parent to a child, or it can arise with a new gene mutation. Normally, the gene gives rise to a protein that is important in several different body tissues. When the protein is not made correctly because of the mutation, TSC is the result.

Tuber-like, noncancerous tumors that develop in the skin, kidney, heart, brain, and lungs are the primary sign of TSC. Epilepsy is common. Although this condition is usually diagnosed early in life, some people aren't diagnosed until well into adulthood. Along with the tumors and other physical effects, people with TSC can have neurobehavioral diagnoses, including autism.

The collective term to describe the diagnoses that often accompany TSC is *TSC-associated neuropsychiatric disorders* (Vanclooster et al., 2022). The features within the TAND label, however, may show up at different ages. Impulsivity is associated with early childhood and depression and anxiety are associated with later years. Autism likely gets the most attention as a commonly co-occurring TAND condition.

People with fragile X syndrome (FXS) usually are assigned male at birth, although a small number of people assigned female at birth can have the condition. The relevant genetic anomaly lies on the X chromosome, in a gene that helps produce a protein called fragile X messenger ribonucleoprotein 1 (or, more simply, FMR1), which contributes to brain development.

Inherited disruptions in this genetic material lead to FXS, which can include developmental delay, learning disabilities, and social communication difficulties. As you can see from that list, these features also are often present in autistic people. People born with an affected X chromosome and no second X chromosome as compensation (in other words, males) often also have intellectual disability. Intellectual disability is rarer in people with two X chromosomes but only one with the FXS genes. The prevalence of FXS is 1–1.4 per 10,000 people (Hunter et al., 2014).

Much like autism, FXS involves features on a spectrum, depending on several factors. The affected genes are called *fragile* because under a high-powered microscope, they can look frayed or nearing a breaking point on the chromosome.

People with the FXS-related genetic material can still have other FXS-related conditions, which are usually detected in adulthood. These include fragile X tremor-ataxia syndrome and fragile X primary ovarian insufficiency (FXPOI; Fink et al., 2018). Fragile X tremor-ataxia syndrome usually appears in older men, whereas FXPOI disrupts the menstrual cycle and has other effects before the age of 40 years. It has, however, been diagnosed in people in their teens and 20s.

FXPOI is linked to early menopause and infertility. About 12% to 28% of people who are carriers of the FXS genes experience FXPOI (National Institute of Child Health and Human Development, 2021). Although the genetic cause of FXPOI cannot yet be directly treated, symptoms such as hot flashes can be addressed and fertility planning can begin (National Institute of Child Health and Human Development, 2021) once a diagnosis is made. This information is relevant for adolescence because menstrual cycle irregularities can appear in the teen years in about 3% of people who carry these genes, and 1% of them may stop menstruating before the teen years end (National Fragile X Foundation, 2018). Accompanying issues can include mood disorders, such as depression, and bone loss.

FXS and autism overlap considerably. They are shared conditions in as many as 75% of people with FXS (Klusek et al., 2023). Diagnosis of one condition can overshadow diagnosis of the other. Autism in particular tends to go unnoticed in people with FXS (Klusek et al., 2023), and there are also cases of mistaking one for the other when only one is present (Bozhilova et al., 2023).

The upshot is an absence of interventions and accommodations for autism or FXS, which can have important negative effects. For this reason, when a child is diagnosed as having autism, parents are often advised to pursue genetic testing for FXS. The spectrum of features, which differ between boys and girls, means that FXS can easily go undetected. Because of potential effects on fertility, identifying a genetic anomaly or FXS can be important, especially for those who might be at risk for FXPOI.

For autistic people with FXS, some autism-related behaviors, such as repetitive behaviors, may diminish into the teen years, and social interaction impairments may improve (Cochran et al., 2015). Attention issues and aggressive behaviors may also ease with age, and in contrast to trends in adolescence in general, depression and anxiety may stay flat (DaWalt et al., 2022). Studies of children with FXS mostly include boys because of their much higher representation in this population. But some limited evidence suggests that girls with FXS may experience upticks in depression and anxiety during adolescence, in contrast to boys (DaWalt et al., 2022).

Many other genetic conditions are linked to autism or overlap with it and often include an intellectual disability. That can make sorting out autistic features from other features a challenge diagnostically (Bozhilova et al., 2023). Most of these conditions are identified at birth or in the first year of life and often require early intensive medical care, thus falling outside the scope of this book.

Connective Tissue Disorders

One group of genetic conditions that are increasingly linked to autism are the connective tissue disorders (Glans et al., 2022). The best defined group of these conditions is Ehlers–Danlos syndrome (Micale et al., 2021). A broader term for them is *hypermobility spectrum disorders*. This term captures a wide array of connective tissue disorders that all trace to mutations in one or more of the several genes responsible for the stretchy proteins that hold our cells in place. Most of these proteins are types of collagen.

Because so many possible genes are involved with many more possible genetic changes, the symptoms of these conditions and the treatments for them vary widely. Late diagnosis is not uncommon. Some signs of connective tissue disorders are not noted or recognized until a person tries a sport or has repeated injury episodes that raise concern, such as joint dislocations.

Signs of Ehlers–Danlos syndrome or hypermobility spectrum disorders can involve any part of the body. They include dislocations, hernias, scoliosis, "stretchy" or thin skin, easy bruising, and being "double jointed" (formally known as joint hypermobility: being able to extend a joint beyond a normal range of motion), along with cardiovascular-related conditions. Some people show signs in their build. People with Marfan syndrome, for instance, have quite long arms and fingers or dental-related problems, such as gum inflammation. Only a few joints seem to be affected in some people, whereas in others signs are present body-wide (Micale et al., 2021).

People with generalized joint hypermobility can have features in common with autistic people, including sensory sensitivities and motor problems (Glans et al., 2022). Thus, it's perhaps not surprising that autistic and other neurodivergent people have higher odds of having joint hypermobility (Csecs et al., 2022; Glans et al., 2022). Indeed, evidence suggests that the two share common molecular causes during development. Another factor may be co-occurring ADHD, which I address in more detail in the next chapter.

The population of people with connective tissue disorders is overwhelmingly female, including in the neurodiverse population (Csecs et al., 2021). Some of the symptoms related to pain and discomfort with connective tissue conditions can be interpreted by healthcare providers as depression or anxiety (Glans et al., 2022).

If your child has connective tissue signs and symptoms in adolescence that are accompanied by ongoing or exacerbating social communication and other difficulties, you might want to check with an autism-aware clinician to ensure that all needs are addressed. Conversely, an autistic teen with new depression or anxiety and complaints of pain or fatigue with previously unrecognized signs or symptoms of connective tissue disorders might benefit from a workup for hypermobility. With awareness of these overlaps and the potential for diagnostic overshadowing, parents can ensure that autistic teens get all the support they need for optimal quality of life.

Sidebar: Hypermobility and Sports

Josiah had a history of developmental delays as an infant and toddler, but with some occupational and speech therapy, he'd eventually landed within typical developmental frames. He was also an extremely active, possibly hyperactive child, with some attention-deficit issues. A diagnostic workup placed him within the range of an autism diagnosis. At the age of 8, he developed seizures and was diagnosed with epilepsy.

Despite social difficulties largely related to extreme social anxiety, Josiah had managed to gain mostly positive attention from his peers for his ability to bend his thumbs backward at all of his thumb joints. He had one autistic sibling with similar joint hypermobility, a parent with scoliosis, and another parent with multiple early-onset joint issues requiring intensive surgical repair.

Otherwise, Josiah seemed to be developing in a typical way physically until he reached his early teens and began to participate in track. At one event early in his freshman year, Josiah felt his knee pop out of place and then pop back in. The dislocation (or *subluxation*) occurred three more times. Josiah had to quit his sports season and undergo a surgery to repair a ligament that had been so overstretched that it could no longer keep his kneecap in place. His recovery took almost a year.

After Josiah returned to track, his other knee started showing a tendency to dislocate. Further examination suggested that Josiah had a connective tissue disorder. He and his parents had to consider whether to pursue genetic testing, in addition to making choices about his continued participation in sports.

Because children, autistic or not, often don't begin sports participation until middle school at the earliest, signs of connective tissue disorder may not become apparent until then. As Josiah's story makes clear, these disorders can heavily influence sports participation and other activities. Someone with a connective tissue disorder may well need to take these risks into consideration when choosing to participate in athletics. Hypermobility conditions may be more common among dancers and gymnasts, perhaps enhancing their skills but putting them at increased risk for pain and fatigue relative to their unaffected peers in the same sports (Blajwajs et al., 2023).

GI

Every day after school, Mari would come home and, after a few moments, head straight for the bathroom. Sometimes, they would stay there for 2 or 3 hours. Their parents, concerned about the situation, tried to figure out what was going on. They suspected that Mari's lifelong problem with constipation might be at the center of it. But Mari was also an autistic adolescent who needed privacy, and their parents didn't want to be intrusive. Finally, though, Mari came to their mother, worried because they'd seen some blood in the toilet. After consultation with their family doctor and a GI specialist, the family determined that the cause was constipation, which had led to hemorrhoids and some slight tears that were responsible for the bleeding.

Mari's parents asked them about what they did at school when they needed to use the restroom. Mari revealed that they never used the bathrooms at school for anything but urinating because of social anxiety and fears of being bullied. They tried to avoid using the bathrooms at all because the toilet flushes were so loud and scary.

With this information, Mari's parents started working with Mari on ways to resolve the constipation and try to time bathroom use at home, whenever possible. That meant timing fiber intake so that Mari could efficiently use the bathroom at home before school. They also worked on introducing foods with more fiber into Mari's diet, but Mari did not want to eat many of the foods on offer. The family decided to use powdered fiber supplements instead. After a few weeks, with a routine in place for fiber intake, Mari was no longer spending hours in the bathroom after school and no longer had blood in their stool.

GI disorders are extremely common among autistic people (Holingue et al., 2022). Estimates indicate that from about 1 in 10 to 9 in 10 autistic people are affected (Leader et al., 2022). Among possible explanations, the connective tissue disorders that often co-occur with autism may underlie some GI and urinary tract issues (Blajwajs et al., 2023). Given the role of collagen and similar proteins in holding all of our tissues together, it's perhaps not surprising that they could have sometimes body-wide effects across several systems, from the brain to the gut.

Children with connective tissue conditions have higher risks for constipation, reflux, and diarrhea, which are also extremely common among autistic children (Blajwajs et al., 2023). Whether the potential link between them is a direct effect of dysfunctional connective tissue, an indirect effect of anxiety or other psychological experiences, or both is not known.

Addressing GI difficulties is important for several reasons. Most importantly, they can disrupt digestion and nutrient absorption, cause pain related to GI discomfort, and have negative effects on sleep (Leader et al., 2022). Other factors include social and sensory considerations, as in the case of Mari. Digestive health and comfort are extremely important to well-being and quality of life. But sometimes, finding the cause of GI-related discomfort can be difficult, especially if an autistic person is nonspeaking and doesn't have relevant communication tools. Even speaking autistic people can have difficulty communicating about what's causing them discomfort or distress (Holingue et al., 2021).

Researchers at Johns Hopkins and Harvard Universities have identified some patterns that can hint at specific GI problems. They say that irritability, "unusual movements," and vocalizing in moans or groans tend to be associated with constipation, as is pain during a bowel movement. In their studies, they've found that abdominal pain and upset stomach were predictive of acid reflux (heartburn), which can often be addressed with antacids to bring relief (Holingue et al., 2021).

The solution to relief for constipation will almost always be fiber in some form. In 2015, concerns arose about the use of laxatives containing the substance polyethylene glycol because of possible contaminants. The most common brand name involved was MiraLAX (Williams, https://www.autismspeaks.org/expert-opinion/miralax-autism). The concerns seem to have settled down, and these polyethylene glycol–based laxatives remain highly effective and have been used for decades for constipation. Because they can be grainy, some autistic people may resist them because of sensory issues. Other options for constipation include laxatives such as mineral oil and those containing magnesium. Although I know of families that have had success with a daily spoonful of flax oil, please note that the U.S. Food and Drug Administration does not regulate this kind of supplement. Autistic people also may not like the mouth feel of oils.

With changes in routine or where we spend our days, anyone can experience a literal gut reaction, including heartburn (gastroesophageal reflux disease), constipation, nausea, diarrhea, and bloating. Autistic people who are especially sensitive to change can experience these gut reactions if, as is common, they must change routines, schools, teachers, colleagues, or friends when transitioning from elementary to secondary school or out of K–12 education.

GI difficulties can operate in a two-way interaction with nausea that exacerbates feelings of anxiety or depression and vice versa (Leader et al., 2022). GI distress can lead to upticks in outburst behaviors or other expressions of distress. Adolescence can be a tough time, regardless of neurology, and our digestive systems can be exquisitely attuned to stress experiences. It's good to be alert to behavioral and other changes that might suggest a GI cause that can be addressed for better quality of life.

Epilepsy

Epilepsy is defined as having recurrent seizures, which in turn are the result of abnormal electrical signaling in the brain. In the general population, about 1 to 2 of every 100 children are diagnosed with epilepsy (Epilepsy Foundation, 2017). Up to a third of people with epilepsy are autistic, however, and up to a third of autistic people have epilepsy (Besag, 2018; Rosen, 2020). Although epilepsy can be part of the genetic syndromes associated with autism, such as FXS and TSC, the co-occurrence of autism and epilepsy is often unexplained.

The types of seizures autistic people experience are as varied as those among nonautistic people. They can be focal (affecting only one brain area), with some awareness, or extend to generalized seizures like the ones often depicted in movies. There are also the kind that are more difficult to detect, such as absence seizures, which tend to be quite brief and often go unnoticed.

Epilepsy is more common in autistic girls than in autistic boys (Lukmanji et al., 2019). Autistic girls are more likely to be diagnosed as having autism if they have a co-occurring intellectual disability, which together carry increased risk for epilepsy (Angell et al., 2021). The current thinking is that autism and epilepsy share underlying genetic and environmental factors in their development (Zahra et al., 2022). Often ADHD, anxiety, and sleep disorders can go along with them. Indeed, epilepsy usually goes hand in hand with more intense features of autism and other co-occurring conditions and is among the most common cause of hospitalization among autistic adolescents (McMaughan et al., 2022).

Although seizures will present early in life for many autistic people who develop epilepsy, sometimes puberty is associated with the start of seizures. Recognizing seizures is often straightforward because the episode can involve the stiffening and shaking that most people associate with seizures.

Less obvious seizures may involve staring, twitching, or brief loss of attention. Any of these kinds of seizures often last a very short time and may escape the notice of onlookers. These behaviors can also often look like typical autistic behaviors, such as stimming, repetitive movements, or appearing to be in another world. If there is any suspicion of seizures, a neurologist should be consulted. Medications are available that can prevent seizure activity, protecting the brain as well as preventing the distress and potential harm caused by the seizure itself.

If an autistic child has an epilepsy diagnosis, their school should work with the family to develop a seizure action plan. Family members and others who are close to the autistic child should be trained in what to do if a seizure occurs, and the autistic child can wear a medical alert bracelet with pertinent information on it. The usual treatment for epilepsy is antiseizure medications, and a wide variety of these are available. Neurologists likely will start with a relatively low dose and increase dosage incrementally until seizure control is achieved.

When selecting medications, the autistic person's aversions, for example, to taste or pills, should be considered (Rosen, 2020). Another reason that treating the seizures is important for autistic people is that antiseizure medications occasionally result in a decrease in distressing autistic symptoms (Lukmanji et al., 2019).

Sometimes epilepsy resolves by the end of adolescence and does not last into adulthood. Among autistic people, however, epilepsy tends to persist, following patterns similar to those identified in childhood. According to a large U.S. study in 2021, more female than male autistic adults have epilepsy, and it's more likely to be diagnosed in those who also have intellectual disability. It's also more common in adults with both autism and intellectual disability than in those with intellectual disability only (Bishop et al., 2021).

Researchers have found that epilepsy medications are often prescribed to autistic adults who don't have epilepsy, whereas autistic adults with epilepsy sometimes don't receive these medications. The healthcare gaps that emerge during the transition into adulthood may leave some autistic adults inappropriately medicated or unmedicated. For families of autistic people who also have epilepsy, an awareness of these potential pitfalls could support planning for these transitions.

Urological Disorders

As you likely can tell from this brief overview of some medical conditions that often co-occur with autism, an autistic person can have many of them. These conditions can interact with each other, affecting their signs and symptoms and even exacerbating or generating other issues, such as anxiety or depression. It can be difficult to tell where one condition begins and the other ends, if they even have distinct beginnings and ends. For an autistic person experiencing them, quality of life can be a huge issue.

The final system I address in this chapter is the urological system, which involves the urinary, genital, and kidney structures and their function. Problems in this system often co-occur with having autism (Jansson et al., 2023).

At this point, it probably won't surprise readers to learn about overlaps of, for example, connective tissue disorders and bladder and other problems (Blajwajs et al., 2023). The constipation that is so common among autistic children can, in turn, exacerbate some urinary conditions that are present at birth. One is *vesicoureteral reflux*, a condition in which urine backs up from the bladder, through the ureters (tubes that lead to the kidneys), and even into the kidneys. Pressure from the backed-up fluid can distort the ureters and affect kidney function. This condition, in turn, can be traced to the presence of flaps in the urethra that aren't supposed to be there, which impede the outward flow of urine.

Urinary issues are comparatively common among people with neurodevelopmental conditions like autism. Studies suggest that up to a quarter of autistic adults have chronic kidney disease (Clothier & Absoud, 2021), and children with chronic kidney disease are more likely to also have an accompanying neurodevelopmental condition.

Some of these co-occurring conditions have an obvious common cause shared with autism. That's the case with TSC, which often involves the kidneys as well as the brain (Clothier & Absoud, 2021). Being born prematurely is also a shared factor in both autism and TSC.

Nocturnal enuresis (known as *bedwetting*) and daytime urinary incontinence (known as *accidents*) also are more common in autistic children. They may be related in some cases to these anatomical differences. Furthermore, the age at which an autistic person experiences successful bladder control can be well beyond the typical time frame for nonautistic children. Their difficulties with control may be exacerbated by GI and other issues.

These experiences can be especially distressing for autistic children as they reach an age where school trips can go overnight or they are invited to spend the night with a friend. Dealing with the fear and anxiety of nocturnal enuresis in these situations can lead to even more anxiety and erode quality of life for an adolescent.

Matteo, an autistic boy, had a good friend whose mother would invite him for a sleepover every once in a while. At age 13, Matteo was aware that the materials they used at home for his nocturnal enuresis would draw comment from his peers if they learned about them. At home, he used adult incontinence underpants with an extra pad inserted, and a plastic protective covering was placed under the fitted sheet on his bed. Sometimes, his nighttime enuresis would overwhelm these protections and he would wake up with wet pajama bottoms. There was no way Matteo would agree to spend the night with a friend, even a trusted friend, in this situation.

Things got worse in ninth grade when the school year began with an overnight orientation trip. By this time, Matteo had become more mindful of emptying his bladder right before he went to sleep, thanks to visual reminders in his bathroom at home, and did not need the plastic protective covering. But he still had occasional enuresis and still wore the protective padded underpants when sleeping. As the overnight approached, he became frantic about the embarrassment he would experience if he had to sleep in a cabin with a half dozen other boys. He and his parents consulted with a healthcare provider and came up with a plan.

The plan that Matteo and his parents devised was to go cold turkey without any padded underpants or other protection, using the protective covering under his sheet. This worked for him after just a few nights of waking to damp pajamas, likely because he was developmentally ready. They had purchased a special alarm designed to go off at the first detection of dampness, but they didn't have to use it. As a fallback for the overnight, Matteo stashed one overnight pad in a bag inside his backpack, but he didn't end up needing it.

Different autistic people will need different kinds of interventions depending on their status, support needs, and communication styles. Some recommendations for navigating nocturnal enuresis and daytime incontinence are paired with the support needs of the autistic person for the best success (Von Gontard et al., 2022). For example, if the autistic person can't communicate the need to use the toilet, a visual timetable that includes toilet time in the list of activities might be useful. More visuals in the bathroom itself can be helpful as guidance in the steps of using the toilet.

If home-based strategies don't work, consult with a healthcare provider about other possible interventions, known as *urotherapy*. These can involve planning fluid intake, scheduling bathroom visits, and sometimes even medications. Above all, the autistic person should not be shamed. The work of achieving bladder control can be difficult, and most people eventually have success.

In closing this chapter, I want to note one final important thing. Families and autistic teens should be aware that side effects are possible with any therapy or medication, and these side effects themselves can present as medical conditions. For example, risperidone, which is used to smooth mood and aggression, has been associated with the development of breast tissue in autistic boys. It also is linked to weight gain, and obesity and overweight may be more common among autistic children (Hill et al., 2015). Therapies also can interact with each other, producing symptoms or signs that may be interpreted as being autism related when they are actually treatment related. If concerns arise about new or intensified issues, especially when coinciding with the use of a new medication or therapy, be sure to check with a clinician or pharmacist about possible interactions and side effects.

Chapter Four

Autism and Co-occurring Mental Health and Behavioral Conditions

Mental health conditions and an autism diagnosis often occur together (Glans et al., 2022; Lai et al., 2019). About 70% of autistic people have some co-occurring condition, such as a learning disability, attention-deficit/hyperactivity disorder (ADHD), anxiety, or mood disorders. About 40% have two or more mental health diagnoses along with having autism. Sex may also play a role in these rates. Autistic people who were assigned female at birth are more likely to have mental health–related conditions (Angell et al., 2021). However, they also tend to be diagnosed in adolescence or later if they do not have co-occurring intellectual disability.

In this chapter, I focus on the brain-related and mental health conditions that are the most common among autistic young people. These include anxiety disorders, mood disorders like depression, ADHD, eating disorders, and sleep disturbance. It is entirely possible for an autistic person to have some other co-occurring condition. For example, although it is rare, bipolar disorder can be diagnosed in autistic people, as can conditions on the schizophrenia spectrum, both with greater frequency than in the general population (Lai et al., 2019; Mutluer et al., 2022). The overlaps across these sometimes-partnered diagnoses are likely, at least in part, attributable to genetics. A family history of dual diagnoses with these conditions is linked to increased odds that a person will have autism (Xie et al., 2019).

Social communication deficits and restricted and repetitive behaviors are core features of autism. When a mental health condition overlaps with these features, autism can be overlooked. Diagnoses with this potential for overlap include obsessive compulsive disorder (OCD), tic disorder, anxiety, depression, language-related disabilities, and disorders that involve self-injury.

Adrian

Adrian was diagnosed with borderline personality disorder in his late teens. The basis of the diagnosis included his history of severe (nonsuicidal) self-injury (which is common among autistic people), ADHD (a common companion of autism), and depression (another common companion of autism). When he was assessed as a teenager (Iversen & Kildahl, 2022), his healthcare team did not consider evaluating him for autism. His self-injury, which drew most of the attention of his providers, is a key feature of this personality disorder, and that guided their diagnostic decisions.

Yet Adrian had a history of delayed language development. He told his healthcare providers that his learning difficulties made him feel "stupid" because he "could not read or write like other kids in school." As he entered adolescence, he showed symptoms of both depression and anxiety. His severe self-injury led more than once to temporary placement in a psychiatric ward. He had a history of suicide attempts as well. At age 18, Adrian was diagnosed with borderline personality disorder. A diagnosis of this disorder is based on several features, including emotional volatility, problematic social relationships, and self-esteem issues. It is also associated with self-harm and explosive emotions.

A few years later, Adrian was given an autism questionnaire to complete, but his score fell under the threshold for an autism diagnosis. This testing was the only attempt to assess Adrian for autism. On cognitive testing, Adrian scored in the low-average range. Despite his struggles, he had a girlfriend and two other friends, although he lived alone.

He described his contacts with mental health professionals as largely focused on his self-harm (cutting) and said that he felt that they did not hear or acknowledge him. That changed with his most recent admission to a ward. A team of clinicians who later wrote about Adrian's case for a medical journal decided to dig a little deeper into his history. They conducted several assessments and included information from his family and others in their evaluations, in addition to directly observing Adrian.

At this point, Adrian was in his early 20s. He had gone through most of his adolescence with diagnoses of borderline personality disorder, ADHD, and dyslexia. The clinical team assessed Adrian for autism in several ways, including using one questionnaire intended especially for autistic people with mental health–related disorders (Helverschou et al., 2009). The results confirmed attention deficit disorder and depression, but not a personality disorder. Instead, the findings indicated that Adrian had autism. This diagnosis had been undetected because his self-injury behaviors had turned his providers' attention elsewhere.

In interviews during these assessments, the clinicians realized that Adrian struggled to identify and name emotions. His self-harm seemed to be related to anxiety about impending conflict. His way of dealing with people was to withdraw and let things "fade out." He showed little flexibility in using different social strategies in different situations. Instead, he tended to stick with the same approaches no matter what.

His parents reported that some of the behaviors listed on one autism scale had intensified when Adrian entered adolescence. A program was begun to support Adrian in reducing stress on himself, establishing a healthy daily routine, identifying his emotions, and reaching out to professionals when he felt anxious. With this program, Adrian felt improvement. The clinicians adapted information about autism and depression into a booklet for Adrian to use to learn about emotions and ways to manage them.

The researchers writing about Adrian concluded that his case was not unusual. They noted, "Autistic individuals without intellectual disabilities are sometimes not diagnosed until adolescence (or) adulthood" (Iversen & Kildahl, 2022). Mental health problems may result in young autistic people like Adrian being referred to the wrong services or even misdiagnosed. In such cases, young people may be referred for the overshadowing mental health diagnosis noted by the doctors and not for autism. This problem may arise because features of autism are confused with those of a psychiatric disorder. Iversen and Kildahl (2022) concluded that, as a result, the "autism characteristics . . . may not always be recognized" (p. 2).

In Adrian's case, his triad of self-injury, depression, and attention deficit in adolescence led to the personality disorder diagnosis. The presence of self-injury and the fact that he almost always saw professionals when he was in crisis turned clinicians toward the diagnosis of borderline personality disorder and away from consideration of autism.

The co-occurrence of mental health–related conditions with autism is a serious concern because of potential diagnostic overshadowing and diagnostic confusion. An autistic person can receive the wrong treatment and accommodations, without consideration for their autism, or no treatment at all. As Adrian's case illustrates, intensification of behaviors can go hand in hand with adolescence.

Mental Health

It's not impossible for a person to have autism and to also have a personality disorder, but many other conditions are likelier companions of an autistic mind. Anxiety, depression, OCD, ADHD, and oppositional defiant disorder are the most common (McCauley et al., 2020). The top three are ADHD and depression, as in Adrian's case, and anxiety (Glans et al., 2022). Any one of these can overshadow autism, given the considerable overlap among them. That's one reason to be alert to the possibility of co-occurrence. Another factor is age. Risk for various mental health issues can shift with age, including from childhood to adolescence, and autistic people are no exception. Autistic people with a mental health condition can also present in subtly different ways from nonautistic people with the same mental health diagnosis. Behaviors and cognitive processing related to autism may be factors in these differences (McCauley et al., 2020).

When an autistic person also has a mental health diagnosis, they can be at increased risk for worse quality of life and greater social communication difficulties. A person doesn't have to have autism to find social communication tough when they have depression, anxiety, or ADHD. So it's not surprising that an autistic person with any of these conditions would find that things are getting worse. Adolescence is notoriously troublesome for social learning and understanding. It is a trial by fire that can leave anyone bewildered and confused. Having a couple of diagnoses associated with impairments can deepen the confusion and affect quality of life.

ADHD and autism are probably something like neurodevelopmental first cousins. The two may be present together in as many as 81% of autistic children (Lecavalier et al., 2019). Anxiety is also quite common, though. It can be difficult to distinguish among ADHD, autism, and anxiety in children. The distinction matters because the treatments and supports for each are quite different.

Anxiety is a fear that is out of proportion to what is perceived as threatening. With chronic anxiety, this experience can be lifelong. Anxiety is extremely common among autistic people, occurring in almost half of autistic children and teens, with similar rates among adults. The lifetime prevalence of anxiety among autistic people has been estimated at 42%. That means that almost one in two autistic people will have co-occurring anxiety sometime during their lives (Hollocks et al., 2019).

Depression is also common for autistic people, affecting as many as 4 in 10 autistic adults (Hollocks et al., 2019). Rates of depression among autistic children start to climb with entry into adolescence (McCauley et al., 2020). Many of the mental health–related conditions that can accompany autism affect males and females in the same way (Angell et al., 2021), but depression is an exception: Autistic people who were assigned female at birth are more likely to develop depressive symptoms (Gotham et al., 2015).

Next, I look at some of the more common co-occurring mental health and neurodevelopmental conditions for autistic people, especially their patterns of symptom manifestation and severity as they relate to adolescence. Although I may mention potential therapies and steps in a diagnostic workup, please consult with a qualified clinician about any concerns.

Sidebar: The Connective Tissue Connection

As I discussed in the previous chapter, connective tissue conditions can be common among autistic people and are associated with medical issues that overlap with autism. A mental health diagnosis can also form a triad with autism and connective tissue disorders. People with hypermobility may experience joint instability and pain, often body-wide. Not surprisingly, pain itself is associated with mental health difficulties. In addition, general joint hypermobility is linked to increased odds for anxiety disorders, including social phobia and anxiety about being injured. Attention-deficit/hyperactivity disorder may be more common among people with connective tissue conditions, and eating disorders may be associated with these diagnoses as well (Blajwajs et al., 2023). Some of these conditions can intensify or first manifest during adolescence.

Anxiety Disorders

The general term *anxiety* can mean anything from sporadic stress about an acute event to chronic, humming anxiety day in and day out. Anxiety disorders have different manifestations and triggers, and the *Diagnostic and Statistical Manual of Mental Disorders* delineates six of them: separation anxiety disorder, specific phobia, social anxiety disorder, generalized anxiety disorder, panic disorder, and agoraphobia.

More than a third of autistic people may be affected by specific phobia and generalized anxiety disorder. Although autistic children can have fairly standard presentations of anxiety disorders, they also may express anxiety in ways that are specific to having autism (Kildahl et al., 2020). Autistic children who score in the average or higher range on cognitive testing are more likely to show standard symptoms of anxiety disorders.

For nonspeaking autistic young people or those with intellectual disability, expressing anxiety and its causes can be difficult. In this group of children, what onlookers describe as "challenging behaviors" can be signs of anxiety and should merit a closer look. Self-injurious behavior (SIB) can sometimes (but not always) indicate anxiety. Anxiety-related triggers for SIBs in autistic people can include surprise changes in routine that disrupt the flow of the day, among others. An uptick in autism-specific behaviors, such as restrictive and repetitive behaviors, seems to predict anxiety in autistic children as they approach the teen years (Baribeau et al., 2020).

A Case Study Involving Intellectual Disability, Anxiety, and Autism

Philip is a young autistic man with intellectual disability and anxiety who was described in a case study published in 2020 (Baribeau et al., 2020). Clinicians reported first seeing Philip when he was 16. He used "extensive" echolalia (echoing the speech/words of others) to communicate, and the people who were trying to interpret his communication were struggling to do so.

The key issue was Philip's SIBs, which were severe but had eased with attempted treatments. Philip had been diagnosed as having autism when he was 4. But his intellectual disability diagnosis had undergone an unusual evolution. It was deemed moderate during his mid-childhood but considered severe when he was 14 years old. Since age 10, he had often lived in a facility rather than at home, and at age 14, he'd been switched from one facility to another.

His SIBs occurred dozens of times each day, usually in the form of banging his head. If someone attempted to interrupt a SIB, Philip would strike out or try to bite them. Unfortunately, the response in the facility where he lived was for two or three caregivers to immobilize him face down on a mat until his agitation settled.

Just before Philip turned 14, he had gone into a withdrawal. Professionals tried to address it by prompting Philip to complete activities of daily living. During this time, his SIBs, which had begun when he was young with wrist biting, escalated to head banging on hard surfaces. Unsuccessful interventions included applied behavioral analysis and punishment-based approaches. Philip's SIBs worsened through all of these attempts. No one had conducted a psychiatric assessment of the boy, yet he had been prescribed antipsychotics, benzodiazepines, and antiepileptics, all to little effect.

The clinicians describing the case initiated an assessment. They administered a thorough series of screens and tests, including questionnaires tailored for autistic people, which Philip's caregivers and parents completed. The results suggested that Philip was or had been experiencing depression and anxiety. No specific event could be identified as causing posttraumatic stress disorder, but the doctors concluded that his background and changes in his living arrangements could have caused trauma.

Careful observation of Philip throughout his day revealed several indications that he was feeling panicky, anxious, and afraid. Every one of his SIB episodes was preceded by these behaviors. He even had physical signs, such as dilated pupils and sweating. Careful consideration of factors that were present during these high-anxiety periods highlighted an important finding: They seemed to develop when Philip had to wait for something—food, an anticipated object, or an activity—and someone unfamiliar was going to be involved.

Philip was diagnosed with mixed anxiety disorder, a category of anxiety listed in the World Health Organization's *International Classification of Diseases*. With the understanding that Philip was especially anxious about uncertainty, people in his facility made many changes in how they reacted to his SIBs. They tried to help him develop ways to manage his anxiety that didn't involve SIBs. The goal was to help Philip get through an anxiety episode without engaging in SIB, which could open the door to decreasing his anxiety overall.

One approach was to time the various interventions so that they occurred right when Philip seemed to be getting agitated. Some of the interventions were diversions, such as suggesting a walk, looking at a book he liked, tossing him a ball that he could return, or offering him snacks. There were other important changes, like shortening how long he had to wait for things and not pinning him to the floor during SIBs. Instead, someone would sit with him on a couch and place a bean bag on his legs until he felt calmer. These tactics led to reduced anxiety and a reduction in SIBs in a short time.

In Philip's case, the association of SIBs with autism overshadowed the link between SIBs and intense anxiety. Some clinicians may have even mistakenly believed that a person with severe intellectual disability and limited verbal expression would not have enough self-insight to develop an anxiety disorder (Winder-Patel et al., 2022).

But Philip was showing anxiety in a very autistic-like way. It took aware and thoughtful clinicians who were willing to invest the time to tease out the anxiety diagnosis and the triggers for Philip's episodes. Especially meaningful was eliminating the traumatic experience of being pinned to the floor by two or three people during anxiety-driven SIB episodes. The researchers wrote that Philip even started to demonstrate verbally and nonverbally that he wanted a caregiver to go with him to the couch to help him manage his rising agitation.

As Philip's case also illustrates, autistic people with intellectual disability may present with anxiety differently from those who do not have intellectual disability. Caregivers and clinicians need to be alert for such differences (McCauley et al., 2020). In light of the increased risk of anxiety during adolescence, withdrawal, increased SIBs, or intensified core autistic features may be red flags that something more is going on. This is especially the case for young people with intellectual disability or for those who are nonspeaking (McCauley et al., 2020).

A special diagnostic manual exists for people with intellectual disability, called the *Diagnostic Manual—Intellectual Disability* (National Association for the Dually Diagnosed, 2018). It allows for adaptations related to diagnosing various mental health conditions in people with intellectual disability (Winder-Patel et al., 2022).

> ## Sidebar: Obsessive-Compulsive Disorder and Tic Disorder
>
> Obsessive-compulsive disorder (OCD) and anxiety often go hand in hand. The intrusive thoughts or disrupted comfort that come with OCD can generate strong anxiety, which in turn can feed the symptoms of OCD. OCD is not uncommon in young autistic people (Martin et al., 2020), and both how it manifests and how it is distinct from autistic features can be complicated. Core features of autism, especially repetitive behaviors, can be confused with or mask symptoms of OCD. Even on its own, OCD can be tough to manage. A combination of cognitive behavioral therapy, which focuses on identifying negative thinking patterns and behaviors and redirecting them, and medication is often part of the treatment plan.
>
> Tic disorder also may be more common in autistic people than in nonautistic people (Wolicki et al., 2019). I place it here for discussion because perhaps the best known tic-related condition, Tourette syndrome, is often treated as a psychiatric condition. Like autism, attention-deficit/hyperactivity disorder, and many other neurodevelopmental conditions, tics have a strong inherited component (Wang et al., 2023). In fact, tic disorder often occurs together with OCD and attention-deficit/hyperactivity disorder, forming a triad for people with Tourette syndrome. Unlike some other conditions discussed here, tic disorder may peak before puberty and ease up somewhat during adolescence (Coffey and Luber, 2019).
>
> Some features of autism can be confused with or overlap with tic disorder. As an example, it may be difficult to tell the difference between a vocal tic with no communication intent and the echolalia that autistic people may use to convey specific concepts (Xie et al., 2023). Similarly, movement-related tics can differ from the self-soothing "stim" movements autistic people may rely on to express joy or ease anxiety, but this may not be obvious to an observer.

Anxiety Disorders, Continued

People reading this may be wondering why, exactly, anxiety is so common for autistic people. Many explanations have been proposed, and the link may have multiple causes. For example, difficulty identifying and regulating emotions can contribute to heightened anxiety. But this example also illustrates a key difficulty in cause versus effect: Anxiety can also worsen difficulties with regulating emotions.

Some experts believe that social communication difficulties are a key factor. Human communication is a mix of facial expressions, gestures, voice, tone, and volume, in addition to words. Working out the meaning in context can be overwhelming and anxiety provoking. This is especially true when factoring in how to respond, make eye contact, and gesture.

The absence of clear "rules" of communication and the constantly shifting ground just add to the uncertainty, and that uncertainty becomes something to avoid. Difficulty with uncertainty is linked to increased anxiety in autistic people (Wigham et al., 2015). Autistic scientist and author Temple Grandin once compared wading into social engagement with nonautistic people to being a novice skier barreling down a black diamond slope: "Sheer panic and no skill set to handle the interaction," she wrote in her book, *The Unwritten Rules of Social Relationships*.

Anxiety about uncertainty and any resulting intolerance can lead to avoidance, which reinforces fears and causes anxiety to snowball. The need for routine can become profound and border on compulsion. Without support, an autistic person may not be able to develop the coping skills they need. That's one reason why it is important to recognize and address anxiety in autistic people—and to try to determine the underlying causes and triggers, as the clinicians did in Philip's case.

Take the common example of an autistic student who doesn't want to talk in class. The reluctance may begin with not wanting to ask for help because the autistic person is unsure about the "right" timing and words. Eventually, that reluctance snowballs into intense fear about speaking in class at all. In an autistic person, this could be mistaken for selective mutism when, in reality, it is caused by crushing anxiety.

Once triggers are known, steps can be taken to address the problem, including visual supports or schedules showing each part of the process. For a student who fears speaking in class, a visual schedule can begin with, "Are the students having independent work time? If yes, OK to raise a hand." This visual guidance can help an autistic student confirm that the time is right to ask for help. Or the student could have a list to consult about the OK times to raise a hand.

As with anyone, autistic or not, clear rules to guide behavior can sand the edges from uncertainty. When they do not feel anxious, an autistic teen can stretch a little out of their comfort zone. Making an environment largely predictable without rigidity can help to strike the right balance.

If anxiety is pervasive and the attempts to address triggers don't help, a healthcare provider should be consulted. Treatments for anxiety can consist of cognitive behavioral therapy to develop self-awareness about symptoms, emotions, and triggers, as well as healthy coping mechanisms. Other types of intervention include exposure-related therapies (such as incrementally participating in ordering a meal in a restaurant until the individual can engage in the entire interaction independently), mindfulness, medications, or a combination of options.

For autistic people, coping interventions that incorporate specific interests and activities can be effective. For example, for a huge fan of snakes, an emotion-recognition chart could show a sleepy, sunning snake for "Relaxed," an alert and wary-looking snake for "Some worry," and a snake in strike mode for "Anxious!" The autistic teen could use the chart to identify and indicate their feelings. To develop a calming routine, the autistic person could think of three of their favorite snakes as they take a deep breath in and then spell the name of each snake as they breathe out. They could do this exercise a specific number of times as part of the routine.

Depression

> "I should expect depression in autism."
>
> —Autism expert

At about age 12, Julian, an autistic boy, had become increasingly resistant to attending school. The situation had become difficult enough for the school to suggest in-home education because Julian had become verbally hostile when pressured to attend school. He was also refusing to do homework and household chores, his hygiene and self-care had faltered, and he manifested considerable social anxiety. Finally, at age 16, Julian was seen by an autism-experienced clinician who assessed him. The expert diagnosed him with chronic, persistent depression. Interventions that Julian undertook eventually resulted in better quality of life and functioning for him, and he was able to avoid being isolated at home for schooling.

Julian had spent years with chronic but unrecognized depression. One reason was that his autistic features, including limited facial expressions and a language delay, had overshadowed symptoms of his mood condition. Yet adolescence is commonly recognized as a time of increased risk for depression, as well as anxiety. Autistic teens are no exception. In fact, they are at greater risk for a depression diagnosis in adulthood, possibly even more so for those with average or higher cognitive test scores (Rai et al., 2018). Some studies indicate that autistic people with depression symptoms experience a peak of these symptoms just before they age into adulthood (McCauley et al., 2020).

Screeners and other tools may not adequately assess non-speaking autistic people or people with intellectual disability for depression, however. Evidence also suggests a sex-based difference in depression risk during adolescence among autistic teens, although girls who do not have intellectual disability may be underrepresented in studies. Depression does have a genetic contribution, but genetics cannot fully explain the increased depression risk in autistic people (Rai et al., 2018).

These vulnerabilities call for attention to possible depression symptoms so that interventions can be started before the mood disorder grows deep roots. As with anxiety, adolescence can trigger an onset or exacerbation of symptoms because of discomfort and uncertainty about the intense social milieu that is typical of teens. Other factors include increasing awareness of differences from peers and resulting isolation from them, greater academic pressures, and more (and even more subtle) exposure to bullying and teasing.

For young autistic people, anxiety or depression can interfere with acquiring important social skills, which in turn can exacerbate these conditions (McCauley et al., 2020). In addition, they may worsen more quickly throughout adolescence.

Sidebar: Depression, Intellectual Disability, and Autism

The assumption that autistic people with intellectual disability might have lower levels of self-awareness and insight as a protection against depression should be discarded. As one clinician put it, "I must

> assume depression is possible," regardless of intellectual ability. Considering autistic people as being divided into categories of "high" and "low" function may be misleading in this instance. That is especially so when you consider that many autistic people may be better at receptive language—understanding what they hear or read—than they are at expressive language, or what they can express for themselves in words. As a result, nonspeaking autistic people may understand far more than they can explain about their self-awareness and self-insight.

Another common myth about autistic people is that they lack interest in being social. The result is that the social difficulties that intensify during adolescence can be dismissed or overlooked. Darius described his experience with two autistic brothers: One had language and academic delays and the other was at grade level with developmentally typical verbal skills. Counterintuitively, perhaps, it was the brother with the greater social drive who had the language and academic delays. His interest in social interaction could leave him the more vulnerable of the two to social confusion or rejection. As I discuss in the next chapter, anxiety, especially social anxiety, and depression can be related to social motivation and functioning.

Depression, eating disorders, and anxiety are all considered what is known as *internalizing disorders*, those that turn negative energy inward, onto the self, often in unseen ways. Nonspeaking or intellectually disabled autistic people may show more *externalizing* behaviors, such as SIBs, when they are depressed. This is what clinicians noted for Adrian—his SIBs were related to his anxiety, not specifically to his autism.

Identifying depression in autistic people can be tough for other reasons, too. Like autistic features, depression symptoms can manifest along an uneven spectrum. The two together can be hard to sort out, especially given their overlap in features. Irritability is common to both, along with lack of concentration (especially if ADHD is also present), difficulty understanding others or expressing oneself, distractibility, and even changes in motor behavior, such as agitation or apparent stupor.

The tools used to diagnose depression tend to be based on a nonautistic population and cannot unfailingly identify depression in autistic people. It's important for autistic people and their families, educators, and healthcare providers to be alert to the autism-specific manifestations of depression, in interaction with other potentially co-occurring conditions.

Irritability should trigger a consideration of depression in an autistic person, especially if its frequency or intensity increases. Depression itself is linked to family history, which can also be a consideration, according to experts. One feature of depression that does not overlap with having autism is a feeling of worthlessness or inappropriate guilt. That should raise a red flag. And obviously, suicidal thinking warrants immediate attention.

For autistic teens whose verbal expression is not fluent, experts say there are ways to ask them about their emotional experiences and mood. Much as described for anxiety, images related to an important interest can support them in rating their mood and emotions. Some parents find visual scales helpful, so the person can point to how they feel. For others, a simple numeric scale (asking, for example, "Where are you now on a 1 to 10 scale?") can be useful to prevent problems. If the number is trending high, the parent can help their child slow down and take actions to reduce stress while the child still has control.

> **Sidebar: Suicidality**
>
> Any expression of suicidal thoughts or planning, or an attempt at suicide, demands immediate attention. Overall, autistic people are five times more likely to attempt suicide, seven times more likely to die by suicide, and nine times more likely to think about suicide than are their nonautistic peers. These alarming numbers call for action on several fronts. Most important among them is prevention.
>
> Researchers are working with autistic adult input on programs for suicidality prevention because relatively little is known about how best to help autistic young people. One project, the federally funded ACE Study, is ongoing at the University of Pittsburgh Autism Center of Excellence. The goal is to use questionnaires and medical imaging to learn more about autistic adults who are living with thoughts of suicide. Another national study into the effectiveness of two suicide prevention interventions for autistic people is under way in four U.S. healthcare systems. One intervention, the Safety Planning Intervention–Autism Spectrum Disorder, or SPI-ASD, and the other, SPI-ASD+, aim to reduce the short-term risk of suicide in autistic young people. For the SPI-ASD, a clinician spends a session working with the young person to make a list of warning signs of suicidality. When these signs are present, the autistic person can turn to their preestablished safety plan and obtain necessary services before the situation tilts into irreversible tragedy.

Other Conditions

Next, I provide a few brief summaries on the co-occurrence of other conditions that are more common in the autistic population than in the nonautistic population. These are all relevant to adolescents in specific ways. For example, ADHD symptoms can sometimes improve during the teenage years, and recognition of co-occurring ADHD can open the door to useful accommodations and therapies that specifically target ADHD. Eating disorders and sleep disturbance are also common among autistic people. In contrast to ADHD, these conditions may start or intensify in the teen years. Finally, claims emerge periodically that autistic people are more violent than nonautistic people and that they exhibit more social aggression, neither of which is true. I close this hefty chapter with a brief discussion of the evidence about violence and autism.

ADHD and Autism

I have emphasized the co-occurrence of ADHD and autism throughout this chapter. They often occur together, possibly because of shared genetics (Solberg et al., 2019). In relation to adolescence, some people with ADHD may experience a decrease in symptoms throughout the teen years (McCauley et al., 2020). This holds true for autistic people with ADHD. Yet there will likely be features that persist, and awareness of this is important for ensuring appropriate accommodations and supports at school. Research suggests some interaction of intellectual disability and low daily life skills with persisting features of ADHD in autistic young people.

The core features of ADHD are in the name: attention deficit and hyperactivity. They must be persistent, or lasting, and the inattention must include five or six of a list of features, depending on age. These features include:

- inability to "pay attention" or sustain attention,
- making careless mistakes,
- appearing not to listen,
- leaving tasks unfinished,
- having organizational struggles, and
- being distracted, forgetful, and prone to losing things.

Also necessary for an ADHD diagnosis are six or more features related to hyperactivity or impulsivity, such as fidgeting, being constantly "in motion," having trouble taking turns, interrupting others, and talking excessively. These features must have been present before age 12 and in different settings (e.g., school, home) and must be sufficient to interfere with quality of life socially, educationally, or occupationally.

As I have discussed, with co-occurring ADHD and autism, one diagnosis may overshadow another. For example, hyperactivity and inattention can be features of both autism and ADHD. Some "motion excess" movements in ADHD can look like autistic movements. But risk-taking behaviors and conduct issues are less associated with having autism and more common with ADHD. Clinicians observing these features might consider ADHD as a secondary diagnosis to autism (Glans et al., 2022). In the case of co-occurrence of the two, autism takes precedence.

In the case of a decision point between autism and ADHD, a child with only ADHD typically shows what's known as *social reciprocity* during testing. That means, for instance, that they usually initiate "normal" eye contact and don't have the social communication difficulties autistic people experience. That said, children with ADHD can have features of autism, including struggles in peer relationships, difficulties with perspective taking, and sensory issues. Shared causes between them may explain some of this overlap.

Sidebar: Intellectual Disability and Profound Autism

Intellectual disability is present in about 38% of autistic people (Children's Hospital of Philadelphia, 2020; Winder-Patel et al., 2022). The proportion fluctuates as diagnostic expansion results in the identification of more people on the spectrum. Autistic people with intellectual disability are more likely than autistic people overall to have other

> co-occurring conditions, including attention-deficit/hyperactivity disorder, seizures, and gastrointestinal and sleep problems.
>
> Intellectual disability is usually defined by a score on cognitive tests that falls below 70, along with important impairments in "adaptive functioning," or problem-solving through the various challenges of daily living (CHOP, 2020). About 1 in 10 people overall have intellectual disability, but it's much more common among autistic people. The disability often requires academic accommodations, which is one reason that it's important to identify it.
>
> Some nonautistic researchers and clinicians have called for using intellectual disability to separate autistic people into different diagnostic categories. Those with co-occurring intellectual disability would be categorized as having *profound autism*.
>
> This proposal has been met with opposition by autistic researchers and advocates, among others. They view it as an unneeded split because all autistic people have autism, regardless of other conditions they might have. These advocates argue that for autistic people, intellectual disability and how it interacts with autism needs attention, but a separate category of autistic people is not needed. They point out that autistic people who test as intellectually disabled may perform differently on later tests, sometimes because of appropriate communication accommodations.
>
> An autistic-run advocacy group, the Autistic Self Advocacy Network, said in a statement that following through with the proposal would lead to harms caused by "functioning" labels, that is, *low-functioning* and *high-functioning*. They note that these labels can overshadow the disabilities related to either intellectual disability or core features of autism. They wrote, "Instead of rehashing old, harmful arguments about functioning labels, we should focus on improving the services available to all autistic people."

Eating Disorders and Autism

Eating disorders have been linked to having autism. The teen years are a notorious risk period for developing disordered eating in general, and it is a known issue for autistic people. A condition known as avoidant-restrictive food intake disorder shows overlap with autism and may be linked to sensory sensitivities around food textures. Research into these associations is still relatively limited but is gaining increasing attention, as are the roles of sex and gender in the overlap (Kinnaird et al., 2019). For instance, disordered eating in autistic men may be traced to different causes, such as anxiety, than disordered eating in autistic girls and women. Studies of eating disorders have historically focused more on girls and women because these conditions are more common in those populations.

The terms *eating disorders* and *disordered eating* encompass a large and complicated group of conditions, many of which begin simultaneously with adolescence. I offer some online resources at the end of the book, but here I want to highlight their association with autism. Research suggests considerable overlap. One study found that 20% of people with anorexia nervosa, an eating disorder involving extreme calorie- and choice-restricted eating, also had autism. Later studies bumped that number up to 30% among autistic adults (Solmi et al., 2021). Autistic traits may be observed in up to 10% of children and young people with a diagnosed eating disorder.

The effects of an eating disorder can mimic some of the features of autism, such as difficulties with perspective taking. This association could explain some of the overlap between eating disorders and apparent autistic traits.

But the appearance of autistic traits can precede the development of disordered eating. One 2021 study tracked more than 5,000 adolescents from childhood, before eating disorders develop. The authors found that people who eventually showed eating-disordered behaviors were also more likely to have autistic traits in childhood (Solmi et al., 2021). Further research shows that autistic people are at increased risk for eating disorders (Carter Leno et al., 2022).

Investigators have examined whether the selective or highly restricted food choices that are common among autistic people might have something to do with eating disorders in adolescence. After all, adolescence is a vulnerable time for these conditions regardless of neurobiology. Results suggest a link between choosy eating patterns in childhood and "later disordered eating." These findings mean that parents and others can try to encourage diversified food choices during childhood to help reduce the risk of an eating disorder later in life. As always, however, food should not be a battlefield, which carries its own risks.

Sleep Disturbance and Autism

Autistic people can have a rough time when it comes to sleep. Teens undergo a change in sleep habits that society often fails to accommodate, such as when schools require early start times just as the teenage brain needs to sleep later. Here, I briefly address some issues, and I have included links to open-access articles with expert-level guidance at the end of the chapter.

Autistic teens tend to wrestle with sleep issues as they transition out of childhood, but about 40% experience improvement as they age (Gavidia, 2020). Not all sleep issues are related specifically to having autism—after all, as many as 3 in 10 people worldwide experience disordered sleep. But it is more common for autistic people, affecting as many as 8 in 10 autistic preschoolers. That's a problem, of course. As a result of poor sleep, autistic people may experience more of the disabling features of autism.

One possible reason for disrupted sleep is the medications that autistic people take for other conditions, such as anti-seizure drugs. If sleep disorders emerge or worsen, that's one place to look for a change. Other strategies are common to all people with disordered sleep: setting a bedtime routine, limiting electronic device usage before bedtime, and being consistent about when that bedtime is.

Violence and Autism

The news media focuses intently on mental health diagnoses when someone commits an act of mass violence or terrorism. Some high-profile instances have involved men who had been diagnosed with autism. As a result, some people assume that autistic people tend to be more violent than nonautistic people. I think this perception is important to address because many perpetrators are still in their adolescence.

Evidence shows that autistic people are not more prone to violence than are nonautistic people. Indeed, in studies going back decades, including among incarcerated people, autistic people are, if anything, underrepresented in these populations (Allely et al., 2017). These findings suggest that autistic people have a lower tendency to violence. In fact, autistic people are as much as 10 times more likely to be targeted with violence than to commit it themselves (Allely et al., 2017).

Some factors associated with violent behaviors can interact with an autistic brain just as they can with any brain, resulting, for example, in an adherence to extremist beliefs that can trigger violent acts (Woodbury-Smith et al., 2022). Other potentially relevant factors may include social naivety and the presence of other conditions, including mental health disorders. Research in this area is ongoing but overall seems to suggest that autistic people have risk factors for engaging in violent behaviors that are similar to those of nonautistic people (Collins et al., 2023).

Chapter Five

Autism, Adolescence, and Social Connections

The biggest challenges many high school students face aren't academic, but social. The same goes for autistic people: Transitioning into high school can be a struggle, for reasons I've already mentioned. Classes can be tougher and the social landscape even more so. Although many parents of teens don't consciously realize or act on it, high school is also the entry into the final lap toward the finish line of childhood. It's a time when teens are preparing for an adult life that is as independent and self-determined as possible.

Much of the energy around the social aspects of being an autistic adolescent centers on "fitting in" and gaining "social skills." The emphasis applies to any adolescent, of course, autistic or not (Rentschler et al., 2022). This stage of life is a fast-moving whirlwind of experiences, risks, and learning to live more independently. Much of that learning revolves around increasingly adult-like interactions with other people who are going through the same thing. Within this whirlwind, a disoriented autistic student may end up feeling isolated and confused.

A Changing World?

In my experience with young people, though, some of this isolation may be lessening. Teens are loosening constraints and are more willing to be authentic about diverse identities and their neurobiology. That's one reason. But the other is that now, a brick-and-mortar-bound life isn't the only place where autistic young people can connect with each other. In the "real" world, schools may offer clubs for neurodivergent students, affinity groups for people with specific identities, or other extracurriculars that draw people with similar interests. In the digital world, social media and online multiplayer games like *Minecraft* have proved crucial for autistic young people to find each other. In these digital spaces, they can enjoy a mutual unforced understanding of each other and create their own welcoming peer groups.

In this chapter, I talk about social experiences for autistic adolescents—what to anticipate in this stage, where strengths and vulnerabilities lie, and how to use autistic strengths to mitigate those vulnerabilities. I look at the problem of bullying, entry into dating when there's an interest, and the role of social media—both positive and negative—during the teen years. I also examine the concept of *social engineering*. That's the planning of social engagement—for example, setting up "play dates"—that is probably familiar to most parents from their child's younger years. This can be transformed into a more mature version for autistic teens. I also discuss school setting—big, small, public, private—in the context of social needs and expectations.

Social Thinking Practice

There are many stumbles and pitfalls out there for young people who are learning to live as adults. Learning with and from others on the same learning curve is difficult enough without communication disabilities that can interfere.

This opportunity is one reason that Timon, an autistic teenager, felt that he got something out of a common intervention for autistic children: participation in groups dedicated to practicing social thinking.

The thing Timon says he liked most about those groups was their small size and consistent membership throughout his high school career. It was a safe place for him to learn, practice scenarios, ask questions, and solve problems. For him, this structure and consistency made it easier to practice general situations with his peers. "It helped me because I could bring up things I didn't understand or that I felt hadn't gone quite right," he says, "and I'd work through what to do."

Self-defense training against harassment or worse often includes preparation practice. Trainees practice common scenarios to be better ready in a real situation to react as safely as possible. Because autistic people often experience social anxiety, an unfamiliar social situation can raise defenses. If there are surprises in an interaction, anxiety can escalate and make things worse. Timon felt that his social thinking group gave him good tools to react in such situations without causing his anxiety to ratchet up.

Timon's groups were called "social thinking" instead of "social skills" because their emphasis was on perspective taking and thinking about the *why* of social interactions. The emphasis was not on viewing social interactions as a time to deploy "tools" in a skillful way.

How are these different? For example, a study has shown that verbally fluent autistic adults tend to be talkative at the same level in verbal interactions, no matter how talkative the other person is (Cola et al., 2022). If social *skill* were the focus, then the tool to engage in conversation would be to simply "talk less," no matter what. But with social *thinking*, an autistic person can think about the specific situation: During a conversation, they can check to see whether the other person's talkativeness matches theirs and adjust their own behavior to match. It's thinking *inside* the interaction, rather than just talking less.

No level of weekly group meetings will fully offset what awaits autistic adolescents. As children age into their teens, they often end up in increasingly larger school settings. What may have once been fairly clear social rules begin to shift. The new forms and meaning, which are sometimes quite subtle, can be harder and harder to follow and interpret.

In the past and certainly still today, a lag in following these nuances can leave a young person open to bullying and ridicule. Autistic people can be common targets of these antagonistic reactions and feel isolated and disconnected from peers (Rentschler et al., 2022). The intensity of these feelings and their effects will vary among autistic people from limited to profound (Pender et al., 2023).

Sidebar: Kinds of Relationships

Odds are that you have never sat down and drawn a flow chart of the relationships in your life. But such a chart might be a useful tool for autistic adolescents trying to understand relationship nuances. Here, I list a few relationships most humans experience:
- family
- friend in real life

> - friend online
> - acquaintance in real life
> - acquaintance online
> - coworker
> - stranger
> - romantic interest
> - friend and romantic interest
> - romantic partner
>
> How to arrange relationships in terms of intimacy depends on their nature. But lists like these might be a useful starting point for talking with autistic adolescents about what is and is not appropriate in a relationship. For example, hugging as a greeting is likely OK for family members or a romantic partner. It probably isn't OK for an acquaintance, and it is OK to ask. It also helps to talk about the expectations for different kinds of relationships. Also worth discussing is the nature of these connections. Some acquaintances, for example, may be people the autistic person doesn't much like, but still has to interact with in a civil way.

Friendships

For many autistic children and their parents, the concept of friendships can seem unclear. Discussions around friendship might focus too much on quantity and not enough on quality. People have different needs when it comes to human interactions. Preferences about number of friends or the intensity of a friendship vary. One person can even feel differently about it from day to day.

Another blurred area is in the terms people use about friends. We can say, "I can make friends," as though creating them from something, or we can say, "I can form friendships," which sounds a little more like the real work of developing a relationship. Making a flowchart of relationships, as described in the sidebar "Kinds of Relationships," can support identifying categories and where the people we know land.

As I discuss more under the heading "Social Engineering," connections that are artificially created with a goal of "making friends" can feel inauthentic to everyone involved. Some of these efforts risk becoming what some disability advocates describe as "inspiration porn." That's when images or stories highlight how some kind-hearted person befriended a disabled person out of pity and, say, invited them to prom. This is not a friendship that formed naturally, but a performance that is especially imposed on the disabled person. It's rarely a genuine act of friending.

If you think about the friends in your life and the friendships you've formed, you'll realize that they mostly did not develop through artificial interactions, like corporate team building. Instead, we form friendships based on things like shared interests, personal similarities, authentic conversations, and that hard-to-pin-down quality of "chemistry" (Campbell et al., 2015). People often know quite early after meeting someone whether they might be a "friend" candidate and react accordingly.

Autistic people can form friendships and want to do so (Rodda & Estes, 2018). Substantial evidence supports the benefits of friendships across a lifetime. Friendship helps reduce stress because friends share burdens, good times, and memories, and they help each other to feel seen, loved, and appreciated. Friends also often guide us, both intentionally and unintentionally, in our behaviors and decisions. Friendship represents a key feature of what biologists would call our species' strategy for survival.

The term *social skills* does not capture the give and take of friendship, including trust and sharing. But practicing *social thinking*—how to consider others and try to be a good and fair person when interacting with them—can be an opening to authentic relationships. When we don't intuitively understand something, if we can learn more about it, we can start to develop intuition.

Parents can help by offering guidance around social interactions, including through digital media. As an example, romantic interest can lead to tricky situations for any teen. Parents can sometimes offer useful wisdom and insights about responding to a text or how long to wait for a response. In some cases, a teen may even want to discuss their choice of words as a gut check for how they might be received.

Autistic people can struggle with recognizing overtures of friendship or inauthentic friendship behaviors, being manipulated or exploited, or miscalculating the depth of an acquaintanceship. But that doesn't mean they can't learn signs common to these situations to help them get better at figuring these things out.

The Nature of Friendship

Research and personal narratives suggest that autistic people sometimes think someone is a friend when the feeling is not reciprocated. Even when someone is a friend, autistic people may not choose to spend as much time with them as typically developing children do. Learning to "read" the nature of a relationship and the subtle signs that distinguish acquaintance from friend or even friend from bully is important for an autistic person. Knowing the signs can help them determine whether their understanding of a relationship is shared by the other person.

That said, many relationships are lopsided in some sense. The key to gaining the benefits of friendship is feeling satisfaction about the relationship, with a full understanding of its nature. As one autistic person noted, an exploitative relationship where an autistic person is manipulated and not truly treated as a friend can leave lasting negative effects. Another autistic adult said they wish they'd been able to tell the difference in high school "between people who liked me and people who wanted something from me."

The phrase *making friends* carries the implication that friends can be quantified in some way. Yet the number of friends we each have varies and even changes with age. Some people have tried to quantify what the average is. One analysis suggested that, on average, we each know about 150 people in a meaningful way and have 5 of them in our innermost circle. Everyone else is allocated in wider and wider circles from that center, based on strength of attachment (*MIT Tech Review*, 2015). But that's just an average for the population. Individual numbers of closest friends will vary considerably.

In the social media age, these numbers can be different. A close online friendship might look different from a close friendship in the brick-and-mortar world. Autistic people can find satisfaction in both. As one autistic adult put it, having grown up before the advent of social media, they had a "few precious friends" who made high school bearable. But by their senior year, there was "this brand new thing called the Internet." For them, it was "full of strangers happy to talk to you." It also was the era of dial-up, so "you had to get off whenever someone wanted to make a phone call," an experience some readers may remember.

This person had been satisfied with their few precious friends who made high school bearable. But they also found satisfaction in interacting with people through the wires in this brand-new thing called the Internet.

Another autistic adult, in talking about their high school experiences, noted that during those years, their autism hadn't been diagnosed yet. They believe that knowing they had autism would have been helpful to them. If they had had a diagnosis, they say, they might have received help understanding "hidden social rules" and "how to have friends and relationships." For this person, the social motivation was there. But in the absence of supports, they felt confused and unable to figure out friendship.

Echoing that sentiment, another autistic adult told me that because they did not have an autism diagnosis in high school, they'd spent the whole time thinking, "If I just learned more, I could act more 'normal.'" Trying to mask or camouflage autistic features in this way carries its own harms (Bradley et al., 2021). Practicing social thinking and learning about social expectations, however, can support better informed and successful interactions with other people and even sharpen insight about social experiences.

Researchers have come up with a checklist of recommendations for supporting autistic people during the school day. These are ideas that can translate into other settings, too (Rodda & Estes, 2018). Some strategies are best begun during the early years of schooling, with parents involved to support the child in positive interactions, but it is never too late to start.

Practice

Practice is important because it eases anxiety. We all practice or try to anticipate social scenarios at some time in our lives. An autistic person can practice how to converse with peers or focus on turn taking in conversation, sports, and other scenarios. They can review why "rules" in friendship and other relationships are not always rigid and map the different categories of their relationships. Real-time guidance during intensive peer-interaction times such as recess or playing games can be useful, with attention to respecting the student's privacy and not stigmatizing them.

Social Thinking

Clinically defined social thinking groups can be safe places, as in Timon's case, for practicing scenarios, working out missteps or peer problems at school, and learning within the group how to mutually support each other. For such groups to be truly effective places for autistic teens, participant selection must be made carefully.

Flexible Ideas of Friendship

Another recommendation is to set aside nonautistic expectations about what friendship looks like. Research suggests that how an autistic person interacts with other people is a fairly stable trait (Scheeren et al., 2020). For many autistic people, including those both with and without cognitive disabilities, friendship can look like doing activities in parallel, side by side, with less conversational interaction than a nonautistic person might expect. Or the nature or rhythm of the conversation might vary from nonautistic expectations. I also want to note that sometimes there is an age difference in the friendships between the autistic person and a friend. This is OK as long as the friendship is mutual.

Logistics Matter

Cognitive or other impairments can interfere with a teen's ability to be in the right places at the right times to interact with friends. It's important for parents or other caregivers to provide transportation or other logistical support to facilitate these connections. Similar supports may be useful for autistic teens who rely on assisted communication in their social interactions.

Friendship is absolutely possible for autistic people who desire it, but it may not look the way nonautistic people imagine it. Being with peers and forming and maintaining friendships are activities of daily living. For some autistic teens, common accommodations for mobility, transportation, and communication will be needed, just as for other activities of daily living.

Parents can also talk about specific, common situations and practice responses with their autistic teens. Scenarios might include who to call if a situation becomes uncomfortable. The teen can practice scripts to use if things start to feel awkward. For example, a young person might find a party overwhelmingly loud and want to leave, but be unsure how to get away without seeming rude and breaking a social rule. If these reactions can be predicted, an escape route can be planned in advance. One possible escape plan is texting a parent from the party, so that the parent can offer a socially acceptable "out." The teen can even have a script ready to go: "Just got a text from my parents. Looks like I need to take off. Thanks for having me!"

Meeting up with friends is an activity of daily living. Parents can support teens in the executive function aspects of making these plans. They can help review safe places to meet up, especially for a first hangout, or show how to confirm a time and place for meeting and how to know when it's time to go.

Sidebar: Gateway Through Stories

When Melia was in elementary school, she became very interested in cooking. Her family started watching *Top Chef*, a reality show that features chefs competing with each other for the title of Top Chef. As each season unfolded, the contestants, or "cheftestants," would show an array of changing attitudes toward each other. Sometimes, they'd hug and tell each other they loved them. At other times, the same chefs would express satisfaction at the expectation that the competitor they "loved" was about to "go down."

Top Chef is an unscripted show featuring strangers in competition and living together during the contest. Almost every scene offers a chance to learn about how people interact and an opening to talk about why their behaviors and comments might seem to be in direct conflict. The show reinforced Melia's interest in cooking and studying recipes, which she enjoyed a great deal. It also gave her family a lot to talk about around human interactions: what real friendships look like, why some people say one thing and do another, and why they, as viewers, liked some contestants and not others. For Melia, the experience was as good as any social thinking class. It is worth noting that her entry point into this learning was her own focused interest on cooking.

For parents whose teens will watch with them, television shows or movies can make for great entry points into talking about human relationships. It's probably disruptive to break in mid-show and introduce the subject. But it is possible to bring up questions later about what people are doing and talk about which relationship labels apply and why.

Reality shows do have shortcomings, and some parents may have misgivings about them. But with parental guidance, they can offer real-time examples of the messiness and complexities of human relationships. They show a variety of situations that can lead to discussions of what motivates people to act a certain way and what their relationships are. Favorite books or other stories offer similar entry points into talking about why humans interact the way they do. In addition, familiarity with these shows can give a teenager a way to connect with peers by bringing them up in conversation.

Sidebar: The Anxiety Factor

As anyone who's been nervous in a new social situation knows, talking fluently with strangers can be tough. We recognize the scenario in movies because we've experienced it ourselves: A socially nervous person blurts out the wrong thing, stumbles over their words, or can't speak at all. The universal recognition of these experiences can aid in understanding how an autistic person with social anxiety might find communication difficult.

The fact that anxiety can take off in the teen years doesn't help. This anxiety can affect many aspects of an autistic person's social interactions. They may even have decreased ability to recognize faces (Antezana et al., 2024), which already is more common among autistic individuals than among nonautistic people. That's one reason among many that detecting and addressing anxiety can be so important for an autistic teen.

I discuss anxiety and different interventions in the chapter about co-occurring medical conditions, so I won't go into detail about that here. But if an autistic teen is struggling or overwhelmed in social situations, consider that the autism diagnosis could be overshadowing anxiety.

Sidebar: Sex Differences

Autistic girls may go undiagnosed until their teens because of practicing *social camouflage*. Whether because of societal expectations or other influences, autistic girls who do not have intellectual disability sometimes can "camouflage" as being nonautistic. Common forms of camouflage are verbal fluency and showing more social inclinations (Cho et al., 2023; Libster et al., 2023).

As with most young people, adolescence changes how effective the camouflage is. Resulting changes in friendships can generate negative feelings and loneliness. Although autistic boys and nonbinary children can have similar experiences, research suggests that the pattern might be common for autistic girls. For girls, there is often an increased expectation of mutual trust and intimate communication during adolescence. Autistic girls may not realize that they are expected to share in a trusting, intimate way in turn, and their nonautistic peers may not understand an autistic teen's lack of reciprocation.

What can parents, caregivers, and teachers do? They can be alert to changes in relationships for autistic girls as they enter the teen years.

> Do friends fade out? Are there hints that what looked like friendship was not, or perhaps was even a bullying situation? Because of their ability to camouflage, a subset of autistic girls can fly unhappily below the radar and be at risk of developing co-occurring conditions. The stress of camouflaging itself can have negative mental health effects.

Social Engineering

Social engineering broadly put is the process of creating situations for social interaction. A common example is the planning of play dates for younger children, facilitated by parental or caregiver transportation and oversight.

For older children, the idea of play dates probably does not match their age level. But there are many engineering strategies for adolescents (and adults, for that matter) for forming social connections and friendships. I discuss a few of them next.

In school, where adolescents spend most of their waking hours, a key is to avoid overengineering social activities. Activities at school, including sports and other extracurriculars, should be obstacle free and inclusive of all students. The reasons are many, but in part, this is because it is in these spaces that adolescents can form some of their closest bonds. Belonging to groups away from school can also let an autistic teen be among peers who don't know about them in the same way as their school peers do.

Some spaces have built-in structures to guide interactions and provide ground rules for them (Rentschler et al., 2022). In the theater, on the track, in the arts, or over board games, young people can bond, learn fair play and how to be a good sport, and build understanding about the nuances of social interactions.

This benefit isn't limited to people with diagnosed disabilities. An atmosphere of broad inclusion and acceptance embraces everyone. In addition, removing obstacles for specific disabled populations has a long history of resulting in sometimes unexpected and important benefits for people who do not have the disability. Curb cuts are one example: They are designed for people who use mobility devices such as wheelchairs, but also prove indispensable for those using strollers or carts.

Offerings should be as numerous as possible and take into account the interests of autistic students (Rentschler et al., 2022). A large selection of student-founded clubs gives young people choices and the chance to share enthusiasms with like-minded peers. Autistic people whose interests are not represented in current offerings can be encouraged to start their own groups.

These and other extracurricular activities can offer a social space that is looser and freer than the classroom. That freedom facilitates variety in interactions and the chance to learn from them. This gives autistic teens the opportunity to experience the authentic expression that trust requires and that is foundational to friendship.

Open Homes

Although young people tend to spend most of their awake hours in school or a school-related environment, they do have time to spend in other places. These times can be opportunities for teens to gather, often without supervision, and build trust and intimacy through shared risks, explorations, and other experiences. Research indicates that during these off-school hours, autistic teens are less likely to spend time with peers than are nonautistic teens. This is fine if they need that time to decompress from the day, catch a breath, and regroup. Many autistic people need and deeply enjoy having alone time to quietly disconnect after a socially noisy experience. But if they're open to having friends over, parents should consider opening their home to such guests.

It can be difficult for autistic teens to communicate their interest in hanging out with peers outside school. Inviting someone to your house, for example, requires planning and negotiating new ground with a person who might already be a friend or could become one. Other people living in the home must be considered, as must schedules, or where the visitor might sit, or what activities they might do.

These obstacles and others can interfere with achieving a visit outside of school. Such barriers can keep autistic teens from learning how to set up social engagements, an ability they will likely need as adults. If a parent is also autistic, there may be a disinclination to have people over, which adds another layer of complexity. Part of the parent–child balance may mean actively setting aside this disinclination and opening the home to visitors.

Autistic adults expressed to me that, in retrospect, they wish they'd had someone who could have supported planning for meetups outside school. "I had friends in structured spaces," one said, "but I faltered at bringing those friendships beyond those spaces."

Another adult said it might have helped "if someone had sat me down (and said), 'Hey, you should ask your friends to hang out outside of the initial context you met them in sometimes,'" adding, "but I had absolutely no social life because it did not occur to me to ask my school friends to do stuff after school."

Again, in all instances, it's important to remember that autistic people may spend time with friends in ways that nonautistic people don't, such as playing a digital game side by side or just enjoying silent companionship. Policing how autistic teens spend time with their friends will be about as effective as trying that tactic with nonautistic teens. Adolescence is, after all, universally adolescence.

Peer Groups at School

Social thinking groups are a form of social engineering that, if well selected, bring together young people who can grow to trust and support each other. However, social skills groups tend to be created by default, by pulling autistic students from classes and putting them in a room together. This form of engineering may backfire.

Autistic adults do not recall these experiences with fondness. One remembers that they couldn't socialize freely during these times, which seems counterproductive. They recall that none of the students in the room wanted to be there. Another remembers these classes as "an unwelcome holdover from ABA [applied behavioral analysis[1]] days."

When groups are constructed carefully, though, the results can be different. It might even be preferable for the individuals to construct the group themselves. One expert uses a "speed-dating" format for autistic teens and adults to self-develop their social groups in a first meeting. In this way, those who meet and remain interested in continuing to meet can say so (Rosa, 2020).

---

[1] Applied behavioral analysis is a form of therapy that has come under intense criticism.

Unlike the actual speed-dating approach, this expert might set up a game night, offering a few different games. Participants play whatever game they'd like to play and have some snacks. Those who wish to continue in groups with each other can do so, in an autistic-people-only space. The absence of a nonautistic guide or teacher allows group members to feel a sense of trust and safety, which are foundational to authentic friendship.

The meetings can be held where those who are providing transportation and other supports can be nearby, but remain uninvolved, such as a library. The key to this kind of social group is that autistic people both form and continue it. The engineering is not done by a nonautistic organizer. And it's all authentic connection, with just a little engineering support to pull it together.

Peer Buddy Programs

Another kind of social engineering mixes autistic and nonautistic peers, but not artificially. Instead, this approach builds relationships around mutual interest in activities, as often happens naturally. One such program designed at the University of California, Los Angeles, is called Program for the Education and Enrichment of Relational Skills (PEERS; Laugeson et al., 2009).

In keeping with the spirit of going beyond social skills and into forming friendships, the program relies on blending autistic and nonautistic peers who are engaged in various activities while providing support around social interactions. Adults work with autistic adolescents to develop *ecologically valid social skills*, which means social behaviors that are understood in the nonautistic world.

An example is how a teen might join a group of young people in conversation. Often, the advice for anyone is to "just go up and say 'hi.'" But in the real world, if someone did that to a group in conversation and then just stood there, people in the group would probably find it odd.

The PEERS program walks teens through the steps of how to achieve entry into a group like this without attracting negative attention or being frozen out. The approach seems extremely centered on neurotypical expectations. But developers say that through the high school years and into adulthood, these strategies will likely prove useful for autistic people in navigating a world where neurotypical is still viewed as the default. I have included a link to the PEERS website in the resources section at the end of this book.

Class Choice

Finally, when it comes to finding school spaces where autistic people can make authentic connections, don't overlook the classroom. Different kinds of classes have different structures and peer interactions.

Theater class is an example. Some autistic people are drawn to theater because it is a place where they can perform a persona using lines and guidance from the texts for a play. They don't have to worry about making a misstep in real time. It's a creative space for those with creative impulses, and "theater kids" famously are inclusive of people who find themselves at the margins elsewhere. The arts also offer an emotional outlet, which can be especially important for autistic people who struggle to recognize emotions. As one autistic adult put it, "Theater and music made it [high school] livable."

Some researchers have taken up this possibility and rolled out theater-based programs to enhance social thinking for autistic people. Theater practice offers openings to sharpen social strategies and interact with other people, goal-oriented work on voice and mannerisms for performance, and peer feedback to encourage improvement. Some examples of these programs include Social Emotional NeuroScience Endocrinology Theatre (Corbett et al., 2022) and Socio-Dramatic Affective-Relational Intervention (Lerner et al., 2011).

The structure of other types of classes can make them a respite for autistic people, too. Well-ordered classrooms or those with clear expectations and timelines may be good for autistic people who become anxious when faced with uncertainty. One parent told us that their autistic child likes their Advanced Placement classes best because the students were "more tolerant" of neurodivergent students and would not tolerate bad behavior toward their peers. They were there to learn, were serious about it, and refused to allow rudeness or bullying to disrupt their work.

Dating

For anyone, dating can be difficult to initiate and to continue. For people who find initiating conversations difficult in the first place, asking someone on a formal date can be especially daunting. Luckily, formally asking someone to a dance without preamble isn't very common among young people these days. Young people can spend time together, at school and outside school, getting to know each other before warming up to something more definable as a dating relationship.

Some high school students, both autistic and nonautistic, forgo dating altogether (Orth, 2023). They often view themselves as too young or just not ready for the experience of a long-term relationship. In fact, young people today are cautious in many ways: They date less, have less sex, drink alcohol less often, and take fewer risks in general. That means fewer expectations around serious dating, easing pressure on autistic and nonautistic students alike.

But autistic youth who are interested in dating will need guidance, just like many nonautistic teens do. One issue in autistic circles, at least online, is that autistic girls and autistic women report having had quite negative experiences with autistic boys and autistic men. They point out that having autism is never an excuse for ignoring boundaries. Reading a social situation can be tough for autistic people, and generalizing across different scenarios can be difficult. This means that learning the clear, unequivocal rules about respecting boundaries is foundational to any romantic pursuit, either in the online or offline (brick-and-mortar) world. I discuss the mechanics of dating and boundaries, physical intimacy, and other related issues in greater detail in the chapter on sexuality.

One thing that can facilitate successful dating for autistic people is gaining a broad social understanding through exposure to social situations with peers. It's yet another reason that full inclusion at school with ample, personally chosen activities with peers is so important (Płatos et al., 2024).

If another person has a romantic interest in an autistic teen, the teen might find that flirting and the subtle techniques of gaining attention can be hard to understand. Indeed, these strategies are famously difficult for *anyone* to understand. Thus, one way to support autistic people who are interested in romantic relationships is to educate nonautistic people about effective strategies for expressing their interest in an autistic person. Direct communication, respecting space, and slow, small advances in intimacy are all potentially important tactics for a nonautistic person who is interested in an autistic person. These are widely applicable strategies for establishing intimate human relationships in general, but some neurotypical people find it difficult to set aside neurotypical expectations of subtlety, games, and nuance.

The bottom line is that autistic people do date and can have successful dating relationships. As for all teens, autistic adolescents will benefit from having a trusted adult available for advice about the ups and downs of the teen dating experience.

Bullying

Bullying is always a concern in childhood and adolescence. Not surprisingly, the struggle to navigate peer communications among teens can draw negative reactions, including outright bullying. Autistic teens are more often targets of bullying than are their nonautistic peers, including nonautistic peers with intellectual disability (Beckman et al., 2020; Bolourian et al., 2019; Käld et al., 2022; Lin & Eapen, 2022).

As many as half or even three quarters of autistic high schoolers report being targeted (Rentschler et al., 2022). Being a target of bullying is associated with developing symptoms of depression and anxiety, as well as physical symptoms (Kald et al., 2022; Lin & Eapen, 2022) and suicidality (Holden et al., 2020). Unfortunately, bullying can worsen among young people as they age into their teens (Kald et al., 2022).

Some programs have been developed to help autistic youth avoid becoming targets, including the PEERS program, already discussed briefly. One element is learning from peers how to handle tense situations and avoid being bullied. An obstacle for autistic students can be their exclusion from interactions with nonautistic peers, either because of pull-outs for services or for social reasons (Boulorian et al., 2019). The PEERS program aims to bake in organic interactions between autistic students and their nonautistic peers, within the framework of a structured curriculum.

Factors that increase risk for being bullied as an autistic teen include older age, being assigned female at birth (Holden et al., 2020), having typical intellectual ability, and coming from a disadvantaged background or neighborhood. Parents and school faculty and staff should be aware of these risks. Experts suggest also digging for the root causes of bullying and addressing them, including teaching all students about neurodiversity and empathy (Lin & Eapen, 2022).

If the bullying follows an attempt to be social, the experience can make an autistic person wary, fearful, or anxious about trying again. The result can be an ongoing buildup of avoidance of social situations in general (Rentschler et al., 2022).

Extracurricular activities that offer some structure around the time teens spend together can serve as a buffer against bullying (Rentschler et al., 2022). Participation in these activities means engagement with something they like among people who share the interest. That means they're unlikely to be bullied for their interest itself. The presence of a faculty advisor or other adult can offer relaxed, nontherapeutic guidance and oversight for everyone, not just for autistic people. An autistic person can authentically be themselves without concerns about being bullied.

It can be tough to determine whether a child is being bullied. Teens are often reluctant to share negative experiences out of embarrassment, a feeling of shame, or fear of retaliation. Bullying can go undetected and unchecked, with all of the possible negative outcomes. Autistic teens who are nonspeaking or have trouble communicating about their school day may be especially vulnerable to bullying that goes undetected by adults.

Signs that a teen is being bullied include unexplained damage to clothes or personal items, unexplained missing items, physical signs such as bruises or scratches, a sudden change in willingness to go to school, and changes in mood and symptoms of mood problems, such as irritability. The stress can also trigger increased obsessive or repetitive behaviors, trouble sleeping, or sensory overwhelm. Sometimes, the teen might act out behaviors at home that they are experiencing from bullies (UK National Autistic Society). If anything raises a red flag and your teen is reluctant to share or finds it too difficult to do so, reach out to the school or to trusted teachers or other adults on campus with your concerns.

Social Media and Bullying

Of course, not all bullying takes place on a school campus or even in person. Social media platforms offer and encourage opportunities for drama and worse. They facilitate quantification of "likes," "views," and followers. Vulnerable teens can track, sometimes obsessively, these apparent markers of their peers' interest in them. With easy access to each other and impersonal distance making it easier to be unkind, adolescents can find themselves engaging in or being the targets of cyberbullying, with a huge audience looking on.

The potential virality of anything on these platforms results in a volume and reach that no other generation of teens has had to deal with. The term *cyberbullying* captures a huge array of negative online experiences, from trolling to criminal behaviors and abuse. Studies suggest that as many as 41% of students with neurodevelopmental conditions may experience cyberbullying, while as many as one in seven might perpetrate it (Beckman et al., 2019).

Yet the interactions are still social. Just as an autistic teen can learn how to navigate the brick-and-mortar world, they also can learn about red flags on social media and the steps to protect against the threats. This is important because research suggests that autistic people can benefit from engaging with others like them on social media. They often are drawn to platforms that involve their specific interests, such as multiplayer gaming, specific Discord boards, or Reddit. In the next section, I look at some of the rules of the road for navigating social media as a teen.

Navigating Social Media and Other Technology

When reflecting on their teen years, one autistic adult said that their saving grace was the friendships they developed—connections with people they trusted. What would have made it better was "the existence of the Internet—I could've found a community of people like me."

That's a sentiment many of my autistic interviewees have expressed about the Internet and social media platforms. These are places to find communities, whether it's over shared interests, shared identities, shared diagnoses, or all of the above.

Yet, as the specter of cyberbullying suggests, as with any human-built community, there are pitfalls. Social media can be a space where users stumble accidentally into negative situations. These can include bullying, unwanted visuals and commentary (especially where moderation is not rigorous), and misinformation that can pull naive or vulnerable users into unhealthy interactions and beliefs.

Many parents might want to simply ban access to social media platforms altogether. Although this impulse is understandable, practically speaking, these apps are social hubs. Limiting or blocking access altogether means removing a route to social interaction, the very thing autistic people need more ways to access.

School clubs and other extracurricular groups use these apps to plan meetings, most friend groups collect around group texts (e.g., using Discord), and hashtags allow autistic people to find and interact with each other or to find people who share their interests. Often, the content can be fun and informative. Research suggests that although most teens use social media for socializing and entertainment, autistic people may turn more often to social media for the entertainment value than to socialize (Alhujaili et al., 2022).

The key is to give users tools to keep themselves safe and to engage with communities in healthy ways. As with so much guidance intended to be specific to autistic people (University College London), the suggestions I provide here apply to most people:

- Remember that online is forever. Anything you post is permanent.
- You never have to engage with someone who is behaving in a way that makes you upset or uncomfortable.
- Block anyone who upsets you or makes you feel uncomfortable. It is OK to block people for whatever reason you choose, without telling them first. You also can report them if you find their postings offensive or if you think they violate the platform's terms of service.
- Never give personal information, such as where you live, your birthday, your phone number, or passwords.

- People can pretend to be anyone they want to be online and are not always who they say they are.
- Related to the above, don't ever arrange a meeting with an online stranger without consulting a trusted adult first.
- You never have to stay online. You can shut the app, close the laptop, and take a break.

For many users, autistic or not, detecting sarcasm or an attempt at humor online can be difficult. It is OK to ask either someone you trust or the person in question how their comments are meant.

For parents and other adults responsible for the safety of a teen:

- Educate yourself about the latest and most popular platforms for teens.
- Learn about how moderation and commenting are treated and about the process for private contacts through the platforms and/or apps.
- Gain an understanding of how social media algorithms manipulate users and have a discussion with your teen about these tactics.
- Talk with your teen about ground rules designed for their protection. It's important to respect the privacy of adolescents, so if you expect access to their accounts, that expectation should be made transparent.
- Keep the lines of communication, however they look between you and your teen, as open as possible. That can mean not being judgmental about their use and always focusing on the question of their safety, above all else. It might be useful to label your emotions—love, worry, concern about safety—as you explain why certain safety

measures might be needed or why your teen should come to you in specific situations.
- Encourage your teen to be open with you if they find something they don't understand or that seems questionable or worrisome.

There is a concern that being "too online" might take the place of real-life interactions and friendship formation. One study found the unexpected result that using social media was associated with quality of friendships for autistic teens, with high use equating to higher quality (Van Schalkwyk et al., 2017). The presence of anxiety diminished the association somewhat. The researchers did not find the same link between high social media use and friendship quality among typically developing teens.

It's interesting to speculate that "practicing" and building social comprehension without adult oversight in a somewhat self-controlled online environment supports better understanding of friendship and higher quality real-life connections. In many of these spaces, there are clear ground rules. Users can address confusing situations through appeal to these rules, which can make them feel less unsteady about socializing.

In addition, operating without the sensory inputs of facial expression, tone of voice, and nonverbal communication might allow for a focus on words and how to interpret them. Indeed, some research suggests as much, with one autistic teen commenting that connecting online meant not having to "worry about physical or in-conversation cues" (Reid, 2021). In addition, autistic people connect with virtual friends online and play online games with a social component. They also use these platforms to keep in touch with friends they've met in person.

Yet, as most readers are aware, the Internet comprises the entirety of the human universe. Anyone using it risks encountering things they never wanted to see or learn. There are bad actors hoping to prey on vulnerable users to steal identities, perpetrate other criminal acts, or just be cruel. Because autistic people can be vulnerable to bad actors in real life and online, I close this section with another list, one that's useful for almost anyone. This one an acrostic that spells the acronym PLAY IT SAFE (Center on Secondary Education for Students With Autism Spectrum Disorder, 2016). It was adapted by the Center on Secondary Education for Students With Autism Spectrum Disorder for autistic young people:

- P: Personal information—don't share it. Never give out your full name, where you live, or where you go to school.
- L: Let a trusted adult know—tell someone if anyone asks for your personal information.
- A: Attachments—be wary of opening any attachments.
- Y: Your feelings are important—if something happens that makes you uncomfortable, tell an adult right away.
- I: Information—remember that not everything you see online is true. If you are unsure, ask a trusted adult.
- T: Take breaks from the computer—it is important to take breaks so that you don't strain your eyes and so you also have a chance to talk to other people and do other things. Set a timer to ensure you are not on the Internet too long.
- S: Spending money online—don't buy things without permission. Money should only be spent by a trusted adult.

A: Act politely—don't say anything online that you would not say to someone in person.

F: Friends online should stay online—if someone asks to meet you, tell them no and always let an adult know.

E: Enjoy yourself—play safely and have fun.

Sidebar: School Size

During the teen years, young people meet most of their real-life peers at school. But juggling academic demands with the heightened social workload can lead some parents and autistic teens to consider changing their school situation. Most people in the United States have options, from homeschooling (depending on state laws) to small private schools to charter schools to public schools.

Each of these has benefits and drawbacks. Most of them are related to what the law requires with regard to accommodations under federal legislation. Public schools must provide a free and appropriate education in the least restrictive environment. Private schools generally are not subject to this rule.

In reality, what public schools do at the local level varies widely. A handful of families probably have a largely positive experience throughout. But many families will bump up against issues related to bureaucracy, school administrations, understaffing, uninformed staff and faculty, and school culture. Any and all of these can interfere with educational access and success.

In the best of all possible worlds, schools offer autistic people the maximum possible access to everything that can be accessed by any student at the school. There are numerous reasons that this makes for the best scenario. It allows for self-determination and exposure to experiences that any teen needs to learn and mature. It offers expanded opportunities to interact with peers and form valuable, satisfactory relationships with them.

Although a smaller, more insular environment might seem best for some autistic students—and may truly be—the opposite argument can be made as well. Some autistic adults, in reflecting on their high school experiences, have mentioned the large size of their public schools as a benefit, rather than a disadvantage. As one of them put it, "My school's massive population . . . meant I could always find my people."

Social media platforms expand opportunities for positive human interaction. At school, an environment with more people may offer similarly expanded opportunities. I do not intend to make an argument for school size or the choices a family makes with regard to school. But I do want to highlight that although a school with thousands of students may seem daunting to many, that very size can be a positive if other factors—supports, access, structure, culture—are sufficiently in place.

Chapter Six

Puberty and Hygiene

It seems like most people who've gone through puberty and those who've parented someone through this stage recall it as a less than smooth ride. Autistic people can have difficulties labeling feelings or sensations and communicating them to others. This issue may compound the other chaotic elements of this life phase, including changes in mood, anxiety levels, peer interactions, educational setting, and one's own body, inside and out. As one autistic person who loves insects put it, they wished that they could go through it all inside a cocoon, like butterflies do, where no one could see them.

Unfortunately for young people, undergoing puberty unseen is not an option. In this chapter, I look at ways to accommodate autistic teens as they go through puberty, especially regarding elements of hygiene and management of the physical hormonal effects. I also offer suggestions from expert resources for talking about and preparing for puberty before it kicks in. As the story in the sidebar "Choosing a Clinician" illustrates, no preparation will be perfect because other factors will always interfere with our best-laid plans. But an informed young person and family with a plan in place, who anticipate common scenarios, will generally be better positioned to meet and deal with the oncoming changes.

> ### Sidebar: Choosing a Clinician
>
> The parent of one autistic teen found that with puberty, her daughter was experiencing mood changes and other side-effects from hormonal cycling. A team of adolescent medicine specialists had been crucial to getting the 14-year-old some relief as she navigated menstruation. The solution was hormonal birth control that suppressed her monthly bleeding, along with the accompanying changes in mood and other discomfort.
>
> The mother had gone to a clinic before her daughter began menstruating to talk about how the girl might be supported in handling the related changes. This decision was one of many important steps that autistic young people and their families should consider well before puberty makes itself known.
>
> For parents and teens facing this road, considerations in choosing a provider may include asking whether your family, like this girl's, might benefit from working with someone who specializes in the needs of adolescents. Another consideration is the level of familiarity the provider has with autistic people. You can try to get a sense of how their bedside manner jibes with your autistic teen's own preferred social interaction style.

What Puberty Looks Like

What do these changes look like? If you're reading this as a parent, you probably have a pretty good idea. How a person looks and sounds; their mood, interests, and behaviors; and, yes, their odors will all change through puberty. There are several fronts of preparation for these changes. In this chapter, I have collected them under the headings of menstrual changes and hygiene routines.

Other chapters address changes related to mood, anxiety, social expectations, and school, as well as ways to prepare for and accommodate them. Puberty and adolescence overlap and interact in affecting these factors. As with any group of young people, each individual will have a different experience. Whether various aspects will get better or worse or remain unchanged is unpredictable.

Here is a brief overview of what is happening inside the body that leads to the changes of puberty. The brain and gonads (testes or ovaries, or in some cases, features of both) begin a chemical conversation with signals from the brain. These chemical signals cause the gonads to release hormones and maintain hormone levels within a certain window of "normal." The result is the changes we associate with puberty: Estrogen brings on the growth of breasts, for example, and testosterone leads to a deepening voice. Pubic hair appears. After the hormonal signals trigger the first ovulation (release of an egg cell from the ovary), the first menstruation occurs.

Along with these changes outside the brain, the hormones cause changes in the brain. The interactions are complex, but for many young people, the result is an increased interest in peers, in every sense. One hypothesis is that the hormones that guided brain organization in the womb activate this organization with puberty, when the same hormones are produced. A somewhat related hypothesis about autistic people is that the organization of an autistic brain in utero might set the stage for atypical development during adolescence. The trigger of puberty in turn can intensify autistic features, sometimes in unwanted ways (Spectrum, 2021).

The age range for the onset of puberty varies. The terms *adolescent* and *pubertal* are often used as synonyms and do overlap, but they are not the same thing. Adolescence is the life phase of maturing from a child into an adult. Puberty is the process of maturing organs related to reproducing.

A person can be well into puberty by the time they reach the adolescent age, but it's possible to be well into the adolescent age range before beginning puberty. Current trends are that menstruation begins at an earlier age now than historically. Among suggested explanations for this trend is the comparative abundance of food (and thus energy for puberty and growth) in the modern era.

I make this point here because I discuss preparing for puberty in the next section. Part of that preparation is understanding that it could precede adolescence by years, especially menstruation (Corbett et al., 2019).

Clinicians have different tools for determining the onset of puberty and the pubertal stage. The earliest signs tend to be larger testes, the growth of pubic hair, and, in people with ovaries, the beginnings of breast development. Environmental factors can affect the timing of onset. Some studies hint that onset may be earlier in autistic children (Corbett et al., 2022), although results are mixed.

Some tricky scenarios that may lie ahead for an autistic young person going through puberty and adolescence include the following:

- Growth: Not presenting any longer as a vulnerable child and being larger and more adult-looking can change how others perceive a person's behaviors.
- Sexuality: Puberty often involves feeling sexual and having an interest in sex. For autistic people, these feelings

may accompany communication impairments that can lead to misunderstandings and missteps.
- Mood and anxiety changes: Increasing anxiety or depression can interact with having autism. These interactions were discussed in the chapter on co-occurring mental health conditions.
- Seizure onset: For unclear reasons, puberty sometimes operates as a seizure trigger in both autistic and nonautistic children, as discussed in the chapter on co-occurring medical conditions.
- Medication changes and effects: If new medications are initiated, they can sometimes have unwanted, unexpected, or paradoxical effects that are difficult to manage; conversely, the effects of ongoing medications may be altered.
- Adjustments to hygiene regimes: The changes of puberty bring new odors and textures to the skin, hair, and body and more intensive hygiene requirements. Dealing with menses is an issue for some young people. These changes can be distressing if they represent unwanted sensory experiences.
- Appearance adjustments: Puberty and adolescence are unavoidably a time of changing social practices and expectations. These changes can be rough for autistic people who like things to stay the same (which is not all autistic people). Peers become more observant (and critical) of appearance. Interest in appearance can bring a tension between what is accessible and comfortable and what avoids unwanted or negative attention. It may seem superficial to worry about clothes or hairstyles. But the fact is that among human adolescents, these are subjects of intense attention.

> ### Sidebar: Gender Dysphoria and Puberty
>
> One consideration as puberty nears is the higher likelihood among autistic people of *gender dysphoria*, or a feeling of mismatch between the sex assigned to a person at birth and their gender identity (Brunissen et al., 2021; Russell et al., 2021). This feeling is not in itself a mental illness. It is a natural divergence between body and mind that modern society has the tools to address safely and in healthy, productive ways.
>
> When it goes unaddressed and a person enters a puberty that does not fit with their felt gender identity, mental health can suffer. People in this situation have increased risk for depression and anxiety.
>
> For these reasons, it is important for parents and other responsible adults to listen to what children say about their gender and to affirm their gender identity. Multiple medical associations agree that gender affirming is crucial to mental health.
>
> I address some aspects of gender identity in the sexuality chapter, but I bring it up here for one specific reason: For children who are transgender or who wonder whether they are transgender, the experience of puberty onset can be extremely distressing. For example, trans boys can find a first period to be disorienting if it has been discussed only as something that happens to women and girls.
>
> Using neutral language that specifies the organs and anatomy in general rather than gendered terms can reduce that feeling of dysphoria (Diddy, 2022). If a child experiences distress about signs of puberty, conversations should focus on the source of their distress. If it's social—such as anxiety about leaking during a period—that's addressed in a different way from distress because menstruation itself feels jarring. For the latter situation, low-dose continuous oral contraceptives are among the possible options, as discussed in the subsection on birth control.

Talking About and Preparing for Puberty

The arrival of puberty should not be a surprise. To avoid surprise, autistic children need to acquire tools and insights about what is ahead and how to navigate it. Avoiding these subjects does not do them any favors. One thing that does help with any upcoming change is a clear explanation and predictions about what the change might entail.

Research suggests the benefits of preparation for changes related to puberty (Corbett et al., 2020). No one can say with precision how puberty and adolescence will unfold for each specific person. But plenty of features are common across experiences, as are ways for an autistic adolescent to prepare for them.

Most important is to consider how to best communicate the information. If the child uses augmentative and alternative communication to interact, then this mode will be optimal for talks about puberty. Communication tactics that have worked for other kinds of learning and preparation for transitions should be effective (SPARK, 2022). If your child enjoys learning through visual media, such as video, there are several evidence-based websites that have accessible content for children and teens. I have listed them in the resources at the end of the book.

The course of puberty depends on the state of the gonads—the ovaries and/or testes. As discussed briefly here and in greater detail in the chapter on sexuality, the effects of gonadal hormones are not inevitable. They can be counteracted medically. That may be desirable depending on individual circumstances related to age, facility with activities of daily living, gender, and physical status.

As examples, puberty onset at a too-early age could call for medical intervention. So will painful, irregular, or complicated menstruation; gender dysphoria (as discussed in the sidebar "Gender Dysphoria and Puberty"); or difficulties with some activities of daily living, such as bleeding during a period. Each of these aspects will add up uniquely for each individual child entering puberty. For that reason, the lists and suggestions discussed here are general and almost always require adaptation to individual needs (SPARK, 2022; Vanderbilt Kennedy Center, 2021a,b). If issues arise, a first step is to consult your child's clinician for guidance. Some expert resources related to puberty and to puberty in autistic young people are listed at the end of this book.

General Considerations for Preparatory Discussions and Teaching

- Teach and use the correct names for body parts and their functions.
- Ask a trusted clinician or other credentialed adult for support.
- Look into what your child's school is planning, if anything, with an eye especially to communication styles and any omissions of important information.
- Discuss the concept of personal or private parts, what these terms mean, and what expectations are about privacy.
- Family rules may need to be updated and should apply to everyone (e.g., private areas should be covered around other people and outside the bathroom, no hands in pants around other people, etc.).

Nocturnal Emissions and Erections

- Explain that both are normal and not under conscious control.
- Explain that waking up to a wet spot is normal and is not a sign of doing something "wrong."

- Using appropriate communication supports, discuss the steps to take when it happens; these can include cleaning up, placing affected sheets and clothes in the laundry, etc., which encourages learning important activities of daily living, or using some form of communication to cue a need for the bed to be changed.
- Erection discussions should be similarly candid and clear.
- Discuss with the child what to do if they develop an erection during the school day, including methods to keep it private, such as tying a jacket around their waist, holding a book in front of them, or staying seated until it subsides.
- In both cases, make clear that these are private matters for discussion only with parents and clinicians.
- Discuss obvious signs, such as enlargement of the testes and the appearance of pubic hair, to acknowledge that these situations may be on the horizon.

Menstruation and Breast Development

For children who are expected to start their periods at some point, discussions should revolve around how that will look and feel, as well as around breast development. More detail about managing periods when they begin is given in the next section.

Preparation, which can be communicated through talking, images, videos, or a combination of these, should include the following:

- Discuss signs that puberty is beginning, such as breast development and the appearance of pubic hair.
- Explain why blood is involved and the hormonal changes that cause it.

- Explain that seeing blood on underpants or in the toilet is usually normal—it is possible to use visuals such as food coloring in the toilet to show how it might look.
- Explain that having a period does not mean they have been hurt.
- Explain that the bleeding should be painless and that they should ask for help if they do feel any discomfort because things can be done to help.
- Talk about the products they will need when this process starts and how they are used.
- Explain the expected average timing of the bleeding and that most people show some variation around this timing.
- Preparing to wear a bra is also important because bras are a new clothing sensation and can be uncomfortable.
- Wearing tank tops or training bras can be a way to get used to the feeling of wearing a bra.

Menstrual Management

Some key considerations for a child who is expected to menstruate include the following (SPARK, 2022):

- communicating what to expect before the first period begins
- if needed, developing a "menstruation kit" with the materials and visual or other schedules and communication tools needed to follow the steps of menstrual hygiene
- practicing what to do with pads or tampons or, if applicable, using period underpants, which may be easiest
- tracking the cycle, using digital or analog tools that are the best fit for the child's needs, with the caveat that information stored using digital tools may not be private to developers and others

- making plans to ensure privacy at home, at school, and elsewhere, along with use of the kit and visual guides
- considering the potential sensory changes or intensifications that may accompany different phases of the menstrual cycle and making plans to navigate them (Cummins et al., 2020)
- considering the potential for periods to involve different types of pain (cramping, headaches, breast tenderness) and working on plans to communicate about pain; recent research suggests that endometriosis is more common among adolescents than previously realized, and this condition can be associated with considerable pelvic pain
- discussing the potential for the menstrual cycle to affect mood, how that might look and feel, and ways to communicate about it (possibly using some of the methods described in earlier chapters about naming and regulating emotions)
- talking about blood as the most visible manifestation of the menstrual cycle and what to expect
- establishing what is normal in terms of amount of blood and pad or tampon use; the U.S. Centers for Disease Control and Prevention says that needing to change a tampon or pad every 2 hours or less or passing clots the size of a quarter or larger is reason to call the doctor, and these comparisons offer suggestions for visuals to use in communication.

Some tips (Vanderbilt Kennedy Center, 2021b):

- A line drawn on the underpants with permanent marker can serve as a guide for pad placement.

- Tampons are notoriously difficult for young people to use.
- Teachers and other school staff should be partners in ensuring privacy for a menstruating child, which can mean talking with them about an appropriate cadence of bathroom breaks and being open to the child's request for one.
- A sign of some kind, such as a token or cue card, can be one way for an autistic child to let a teacher or staff member know about the need for a hygiene bathroom break.
- Keeping a consistent daily schedule of breaks can help avoid accidents.
- Think about clothing and whether it will support privacy and hygiene or impede it.
- If menstrual products are hard to remove from their packaging, consider making unwrapped products available, perhaps as part of the menstruation kit.
- Ensure that any adults working with the child in support of hygiene needs are properly trained and backgrounded and are providing the appropriate independence and privacy for the child (Cummins et al., 2020).

A sample list of steps for changing a pad (in part from Lundy et al., 2022):

- Bring a new menstrual pad to the bathroom or make sure one is in the bathroom
- Go into the bathroom
- Shut the door
- Stand near the toilet

- Pull clothes (pants/shorts/skirt and underpants) below knees
- Sit on the toilet
- Remove the old pad from the underwear
- Fold it and wrap in toilet paper
- Put in trash can
- Wipe vagina with toilet paper
- Drop that toilet paper in the toilet
- Open the new menstrual pad (if it is not open already)
- If wrapping needs to be removed, throw wrapper in trash
- Remove paper on top of the sticky strip
- Throw paper in trash
- Place sticky strip on underpants and press into place
- Stand up
- Pull up underpants and pants/skirt/shorts
- Flush toilet
- Wash hands

Underwear is now available that's designed specifically for easy handling of menstruation, without the paper products. This type of clothing might be the best choice for many autistic people who find processes involving paper products too difficult to navigate or too uncomfortable.

Remember that childhood development is personal to every child. That also applies to puberty. How an autistic person will handle menstruation and puberty is difficult to predict. As with all children entering this phase, some do quite well and others experience difficulties with pain, mood, managing hygiene, and communicating their needs (Cummins et al., 2020). The role of parents is to be sensitive to the experiences of their child and provide the tools to support independence in menstrual management.

> ### Sidebar: Birth Control
>
> Some studies suggest that despite parental worries about how their autistic child will manage menstruation, often the troubles they anticipate don't arise (Cummins et al., 2020). But medical interventions are available if the child finds management too difficult or menstruation involves too much distress or harm because of pain, heavy bleeding, severe acne, or other issues (Vanderbilt Kennedy Center, 2021b). Consideration of interventions should begin with a discussion with the child and with their healthcare provider.
>
> Probably the most common intervention is low-dose hormonal contraception. This can be prescribed to lighten a period or even limit bleeding almost completely. It does require taking a daily pill. As with any medical intervention, oral contraception carries risks, including blood clotting in some cases.
>
> Shots and implants that deliver hormonal therapies also are available, with some of the same risks as oral contraceptives. Tolerance of the administration procedure must be considered. Injections usually are administered every few months. An arm implant of a matchstick-size rod that delivers hormone can be effective for a few years. Implantation of an intrauterine device is another option that can suppress or lighten periods for years. It also carries risks, including insertion pain and ongoing spotting.

Hygiene Routines

Becoming independent in caring for a body that is itself undergoing changes is a big task. So many parts require consideration: hair, nails, skin care and shaving, body odor, and teeth. Upkeep of each of these is a multistep process. It's no wonder that taking responsibility for them all can be such a huge job.

One way to ease into these responsibilities is for a child to take them on gradually, in developmentally appropriate ways. Visual instructions and videos can be helpful, as can practice and patience. Like the kit for menstrual management, kits can be developed for other aspects of puberty-related hygiene: shaving, bathing and hair washing, and dental care. Kits can also be made for hygiene practices at specific times, like a morning kit for preparing for school and an evening kit to prepare for bedtime (Vanderbilt Kennedy Center, 2021a, b).

An important part of any hygiene practice is routine. A visual schedule for each day or week can be helpful. If social effects don't gain traction with a child, then an emphasis on good health could be discussed. For example, teeth brushing and flossing are associated with a healthy body, and washing hands can help avoid illness.

It's also possible to create hygiene rituals related to music or something else fun. Examples include playing favorite songs for a specific length of time for a shower or a favorite short video clip to go with tooth brushing. Visual schedules for showering or bathing can be laminated so they can survive soap and water.

For children who want to wear makeup, the first decision is determining what is age appropriate and fits with the family's values and expectations at school. Many instructional videos about makeup application are available on the Internet. An interested child can also practice on drawn or printed images or another family member, which could be fun for them, too.

Keep sensory sensitivities in mind. Many shampoos, soaps, toothpastes, lotions, deodorants, and other hygiene products have strong or annoying odors. But plenty of products are unscented or mildly scented. Parents are probably the ones making these purchases, so it's good to keep sensitivities in mind and to respond to feedback about choices.

Skin care can be especially difficult, particularly shaving and dealing with acne. For blemishes, practicing application on a picture or another family member can be helpful. Videos can offer guidance for many hygiene processes.

The child can also practice shaving on magazine pages or other pictures to get a feel for it. Electric razors may be the easiest and safest to manage, unless the noise or feeling of the razor is bothersome. Likewise, an electric toothbrush may prove more effective than conventional versions for dental hygiene. For each process, as with all other aspects of puberty, practice and preparation, along with a list of steps, can be key to success.

Chapter Seven

Autism, Adolescence, and Sexuality

Education practices related to sex and sexuality are highly variable throughout the United States (Crehan et al., 2024). Less than half of U.S. high schools offer a comprehensive curriculum, and an even smaller proportion of middle schools do so (NPR/Kaiser/Kennedy School Poll). The delivery of evidence-based, accurate, age-appropriate guidance and instruction is even more scattershot.

Attitudes about autistic people and their interests, competence, and capacities can interfere with the delivery of important information about appropriate behaviors, boundaries, consent, and the anatomy and function of the human body. Evidence suggests that autistic people may know even less about sex than their nonautistic peers (Houtrow et al., 2021; Joyal et al., 2021). That is in part because adults may treat autistic teens like small children or believe common myths about sexuality and disability (Coulter et al., 2023).

One such myth is that autistic people aren't interested in sex, dating, or romance. I have addressed this in part in a previous chapter, and evidence thoroughly counters this belief. A majority of autistic young people report being interested in sex and romantic connection (Joyal et al., 2021). They have just as much need to understand their sexuality as any other young person. Another myth is that those who are nonspeaking or have intellectual disability can't understand sex-related education. Neither of these things is true. An appropriate level of adapted education is needed.

Age-appropriate understanding of sex, sexuality, reproduction, and relevant anatomy and function are crucial for all children, from early in their lives. Without this information, risks are increased for negative outcomes. These outcomes include becoming victims of assault, experiencing an unwanted pregnancy, acquiring a sexually transmitted infection, and developing low self-esteem (Crehan et al., 2024). Autistic people are at even greater risk.

Having good information about sexuality and sex—something that 97% of adults engage in during a lifetime—holds many benefits. It offers protection against sexual abuse, is linked to being older at the first sexual experience and having a more enjoyable experience (Crehan et al., 2024), and is associated with reduced risk for intimate partner or emotional violence (Mhatre, 2021). Yet autistic youth are less likely than their peers to receive formal education in reproductive health. As of 2022, only five states had mandated that disabled students have accessible health education (Graham Holmes et al., 2022).

By the time most children reach adolescence, they've had some exposure to information about sex. Often, this information comes from media consumption (Houtrow et al., 2021) and from peers (although parents and schools are sources of guidance, as well). For an autistic person, the peer relationships needed for this information exchange can in themselves be a stumbling block.

The result is that autistic young people with curiosity about and interest in sex can end up feeling lost. In addition, sexuality education is as much about self-protection and self-awareness as it is about understanding anatomy and function. Autistic people who lack relevant information are at risk for becoming targets of unwanted behaviors or of unwittingly offending by transgressing in their own behaviors.

The need is especially urgent to educate autistic boys and autistic young men about consent, boundaries, and private versus public conduct. The "hidden curriculum" of social interactions among young people is opaque to many autistic people. The subset of cues related to sex and attraction is no exception. For these reasons, autistic people (and, really, all young people) need information that is clear, concrete, rules based, and communicated in a way that works best for them. The good news is that no one reading this has to invent materials for themselves. At the end of this book are links to some resources that have been developed with these aims in mind.

An inclination to view childhood and adolescence as separate from sex and sexuality is somewhat understandable. But the reality is that most humans are born with reproductive anatomy. The process of puberty, which coincides with adolescence, is maturation of that anatomy and related functions. Every human should be equipped with the tools to understand what's happening, protect themselves, and behave appropriately with others.

Healthy Sexuality

What does healthy sexuality look like? Sexuality is part of our sense of self and is far more than the act of sex itself. It is key to how we view the world and our place in it. It is central to our behavior, anatomy, and physical, emotional, and mental health. Everyone, regardless of ability or disability, needs access to appropriate sexual health education to ensure a healthy sense of self and related behaviors (ASAN, 2021; Coulter et al., 2023).

Sexuality Education and Autistic People

Studies show that parents and clinicians are less likely to be sources of information about sexuality for people with disabilities (Mhatre, 2021). One factor may be the common misconception that disabled people are uninterested in or cannot engage in sex or reproduce. The discomfort many parents feel about these issues means that when schools don't pick up the slack, autistic young people can come up short on understanding sexuality and reproductive health.

In the absence of other guidance, young autistic people, who are at increased risk for sexual abuse and exploitation (Holmes et al., 2019), will remain unsafe. The social mix of how people view autistic children and the key traits of having autism may combine to deepen these risks. For these reasons, appropriate education for autistic students is even more crucial. Missing subtle red flags or being unaware of the hidden curriculum among same-age peers can give an autistic person at an unsafe and potentially dangerous deficit.

Adolescent peers have long served as a (frequently faulty) resource and sounding board about sexuality and reproductive health. Media consumption also plays a role. Communication difficulties related to autism can interfere with peer–peer interactions that inform, guide, and result in related behaviors. Parents and families have a key safety role in creating a space for being consulted. In this way, they can ensure that information is provided in a way that works best for their child and set family expectations around privacy and behavior (Holmes et al., 2019).

Parents of autistic children who have intellectual disability or who are nonspeaking should not think that sexuality education is unnecessary (Holmes et al., 2019). Parents tend to offer more guidance when a child asks questions or expresses interest. If parents don't recognize such cues, they may not think about having these discussions with their child. Evidence suggests that autistic children have just as much interest in and curiosity about sex and sexuality as do their nonautistic peers, so parents should assume the interest.

Sexuality Education: Why It Is Important

Risk reduction with appropriate education is the main reason to offer systematic access to reproductive health and sexuality education. It should be part of the standard of education and care for autistic people. Autistic people themselves, when surveyed, reflect a need to be informed. They cite it as important for learning to have healthy relationships, for not being lonely, for safety, and to be equipped to decide what is right for them. As one self-advocate said about their own experience (or lack of) with sex education, "I didn't receive any information in school or from my provider. I learned by the 'school of hard knocks.' I am still trying to work through the trauma of learning the hard way" (Organization for Autism Research, 2023).

ASAN has provided information about why "sex ed" is important (Mhatre, 2021). They note the well-established physical and mental health benefits of being well informed and add that this access is a "matter of dignity." Information is power. An understanding of sexuality, consent, and relationships empowers autistic people in asserting bodily autonomy. That in turn is linked to safety, dignity, and independence. ASAN writes (Mhatre, 2021, p. 6),

> Everyone deserves to learn about consent, to challenge and break down stigmas around sex and sexuality, and to get information and resources that increase the likelihood of having healthy sexual experiences. Not having this knowledge undermines our efforts to participate fully in our own lives and communities and defeats our self-determination.

Even if an autistic person is more interested in nonsexual intimacy with their closest confidantes, as many autistic people are, sexuality education is important. They need tools to ensure their safety and autonomy, too.

ASAN also notes that comprehensive sexuality education for people with disabilities should address the accommodations, whether intellectual or physical or both, needed for a healthy sexuality (Mhatre, 2021). A related piece of federal legislation, the Real Education and Access for Healthy Youth Act, was reintroduced in the U.S. House of Representatives in 2023 after a similar proposal stalled out in 2021. The goal of the act is to smooth access to sexuality education, especially for young adults who encounter obstacles accessing care.

If the act were to pass, it would establish federal grants to fund high school and college programs that support comprehensive education in sexual health. The programs would include consideration of different gender identities and gender expressions. If successful, this or other similar measures could address established gaps that autistic young people experience in accessing developmentally appropriate sexual health education and information (Pecora et al., 2020).

Some parents may be concerned that education about sexual and reproductive health and sexuality will in some way "encourage" sexual behaviors. Research has thoroughly demonstrated that knowledge is both power and empowering, promoting safety and safer behaviors.

Sexuality Education: Who Is Responsible for It?

The best sources of information are experts who understand not only the material and related issues but also how to deliver the information in ways that are developmentally appropriate. As noted, parents can and should contribute if they feel OK doing so. If they are not comfortable with it, they still can be available as a "safe" person to consult and ask for help (Organization for Autism Research, 2018).

When parents do engage with their child about these subjects, as always, adopting the communication tools that work in the education setting in general is important. Studies suggest that parents often don't turn to visual materials such as videos or pictures when discussing sex and sexuality with their autistic child, even if these tools are typically used for learning (Holmes et al., 2019). The end of this book contains a substantial resource list that includes videos and other tools parents can use to support this education.

Consent

Sexuality education goes well beyond anatomy and function. A comprehensive curriculum will spend a lot of time on the concept of consent. Autistic people need educational approaches that ensure that they have clarity about consent. Understanding what it means to give consent or not is crucial from any perspective when it comes to bodily autonomy and safety.

A 2021 study of young autistic adults (first-year college students) found that about a quarter of them learned about consent from a website and another quarter from peers (Organization for Autism Research, 2021b). These avenues of information may not offer the necessary clarity about what consent looks like and how to confirm it to or from someone else.

Some scenarios are obvious. But many sexual or romantic encounters have muddy dynamics that, for concrete thinkers, can lead to risks of sustaining or causing harm. Research suggests that autistic people especially would benefit from working through different scenarios that seem to involve "gray areas" around consent. As with other social thinking practice, this preparation can give them a clear reference for specific situations (Crehan et al., 2024). In general, people with intellectual and developmental disabilities face higher barriers to accessing this information. That's one reason that it's important to have experts not only in delivery but also in adaptation and accommodation.

A common refrain in one popular and useful educational video series is that "No means no, and maybe doesn't mean yes" (RockStarDinosaurPiratePrincess/Blue Seat Studios, 2015). But understanding consent may require more than this straightforward script. And ensuring that the other person understands one's own communication about consent can require another element: assertiveness. Autistic people, especially if they've gone through therapy programs that persistently emphasize compliance, may not have the tools they need to be assertive in their self-determination about consent.

Here is some information about consent and what it means: Consent is a freely chosen yes. That means that the yes was given without coercion: No threats, manipulation, pressure, quid pro quo (this in exchange for that), bribery, force, or other tactics were used. Experts say that two questions can be used to determine the nature of consent when it is given:

1. Did the person say the word "yes"?
2. Was the yes freely chosen (i.e., without any coercive tactics being used)?

Yes responses to both questions mean that consent has been given.

Clear, step-by-step processes like these can be a huge help for concrete thinkers who rely on rule systems to make sure they are "doing the right thing."

It's also helpful to use examples, such as scenarios around consent and what coercive tactics might look like. Here are some examples, taken from the Organization for Autism Research (2023). These can be used with picture stories or other methods of communication.

- *Lie*: Someone says "I love you" when they don't mean it, just to get what they want.
- *Threat*: "If you don't do what I am asking, I'll find someone who will."
- *Pressuring*: "Everyone else is doing it," or "[Friends they know] are doing it, it's not a big deal," or begging, such as "Please, just this once, I won't ask again."

- *Intimidation and blackmail*: "I'll just tell everyone you did it anyway, so you may as well."
- *Bribery*: "I'll give you money if you do this."
- *Use of force*: Any contact made without consent and/or with the intention of coercion; this is criminal behavior, including if it is committed against people who are unable to give consent for some reason, for example, because they are unconscious.

Situations often may not be that clear-cut but should always be resolvable by going back to those two key questions. And when in doubt, don't.

What "No" Means

The assertiveness aspect of consent, which is always a two-way interaction, is extremely important to communicate to autistic people. Over a lifetime, especially if they have been subjected to a common intervention program focused on behavioral compliance, autistic people may be primed to be nonassertive.

For this reason, an autistic child may need to practice saying no in specific scenarios, in a firm, straightforward way. Self-defense and antiharassment trainings emphasize the importance of preparation like this. It creates awareness of what to do and reduces the surprise that can disarm someone who is less prepared.

Practice doesn't have to involve specifically sex-related scenarios. It can be scenarios of basic assertions of autonomy, with an explanation that "no" can be used in any situation that feels uncomfortable. It's important to practice just saying no, without following up on a common impulse to supply a reason or excuse or to waffle.

The other side of this practice is to practice *accepting* when someone says no. Young people must understand that assertiveness is completely OK for self-protection but should not be used to get something from another person.

> ### Sidebar: At Risk
>
> Autistic people may have up to three times the risk of nonautistic people of experiencing sexual victimization in the form of violence, unwanted contact, and coercion (Cazalis et al., 2022), often in their teens. Whether girls and women are more affected than boys and men is unclear (Joyal et al., 2021; Pecora et al., 2020). Regardless, this risk increases their odds of negative mental health outcomes, such as posttraumatic stress disorder.
>
> These increased risks raise concerns that communication impairments are involved (Pecora et al., 2020). Autistic people may have more difficulty recognizing victimization and leave an experience unreported or continue in unsafe situations. Autistic people who identify with the queer community may have even greater increased risk.
>
> Although many factors are likely involved in these magnified risks for autistic people, education and information are protective (Joyal et al., 2021). The protection cuts both ways. Naivete resulting from a lack of comprehensive sex education, confusion about boundaries and consent, and a lack of peer feedback because of social difficulties all can heighten the risk of victimization. But they also can contribute to making an autistic person an unwitting offender. Accurate, accessible, and comprehensive education about consent and boundaries can give autistic teens tools to support their decision-making on both sides of a sexual interest interaction.

Boundaries

Boundaries are important in many aspects of sexuality and sexual behaviors. They must be defined on several levels, including public versus private behaviors, as well as the gray areas in between, and the bodily autonomy of self and others. Understanding boundaries in different situations can be protective for autistic people in most aspects of their lives, including hygiene and activities of daily living (Gerhardt & Gravino, 2018).

In the previous chapter, I talked about defining family rules about private behaviors. An example is always having the bathroom door closed when using the bathroom for toileting and other hygiene purposes. Previously, I discussed another aspect of boundary setting: learning how to say no firmly and without exception, using scenarios for practice.

Our lives are full of shifting boundaries. For sexuality and sex-related behaviors, what's socially acceptable for private behaviors is quite different from what is socially acceptable in public. It's OK (usually) to hold hands with and lightly kiss a partner in many public spaces. But removing clothing or touching one's own or another person's genitalia in public is usually inappropriate. These are all sex-related behaviors. Autistic people need accessible ways to understand where the lines are in different situations.

Offenders

The reality for autistic people is that communication disabilities can lead to misunderstandings and unwitting offending. Autistic women have commented publicly about feeling "very uncomfortable" and "unsafe" around autistic men who are interested in women. One autistic expert described her negative experience with an autistic man at her first job. She blames the experience on a lack of consent education for autistic children and the use of autism as an excuse for not teaching about these matters.

She was unsure what to do because she didn't want to harm the man or his livelihood, but she wanted him to stop his behaviors, which those around him ignored. In the end, he did lose his job, and she suffered from the situation for a long time. As she noted, they were both failed by the attitude that no one needed to stop him or change his behavior because he had autism. Clearly still experiencing the negative aftermath of what happened, she noted again and again how angry she still felt, for herself and for him.

Violating consent boundaries through "inappropriate courting" isn't the only way autistic people can misstep, criminally. Out of ignorance, autistic people may unwittingly break laws related to sex behaviors. Autistic people are overrepresented in the population that does so (Pecora et al., 2020).

Research also suggests that autistic people are at increased risk for (unwittingly) engaging in what are known as *paraphilic* sexual interests. This category encompasses fetishism and pedophilia. This subject is highly sensitive, but some cases certainly involve naivety and a lack of understanding about boundaries. The result can be transgressions that include indecent exposure, public masturbation, and inappropriate contact with minors or viewing images of child exploitation.

The latter is what some authors have described as an "increasing point of contact with the criminal justice system for people on the autism spectrum" (Pecora et al., 2020, p. 546). Relevant factors may include spending time online in the absence of real-life social contact and in the face of social anxiety (Singer, 2023). Another factor is having interests that are "developmentally young" that lead autistic people into contact with younger people (Organization for Autism Research, 2023). As always, inadequate or nonexistent sexuality education is a risk factor, not just for autistic teens but also for teens in general (Pecora et al., 2020).

The autistic population at greatest risk for contacts with authorities are autistic men who do not have intellectual disability. Once again, one of the best protections against risk is appropriate, accessible, comprehensive sexuality education. As expert Eileen Crehan, an assistant professor in the Eliot-Pearson Department of Child Study & Human Development at Tufts University, pointed out, one fact is clear-cut and easily communicated: age 18 and over, only (Singer, 2023).

> They may have interests that are developmentally young, so the folks they strike up conversations with may be under 18. If things progress to swapping pictures, there are huge legal ramifications. I spend a lot of time in our groups emphasizing that 18-year-old threshold. The good news is that it's a clear black-and-white rule. If you are over 18, only romantic activities with others over 18!

Finally, there is the issue of what is called *counterfeit deviance*. These are behaviors that seem deviant, like using a nonsexual object such as a book to masturbate. In reality, the object is serving as an accommodation for impaired motor function. One solution is to determine what typically would be used in such situations and furnish the necessary material.

Media and the Internet

As I have illustrated, the Internet can be packed with pitfalls for young users. That's not news to any parent in the modern era. But it's also a place where autistic people can turn for controlled social interactions, finding community, and getting, yes, good information. Social media apps also are increasingly used to arrange social and school-related meetings and activities. Banning them entirely or attempting to severely limit access can backfire in a number of ways.

As with sexuality education in general, the key is to understand that education and information are powerful protectives. Clear rules can also go a long way toward protection. Not surprisingly, they involve boundaries. Experts suggest establishing the following boundaries for safety:

- You don't have to post or share anything you don't want to.
- Online never goes away—always assume that anything you post online, even if it is ostensibly private, will be available to anyone at some point.
- Do not give out personal information, including your address, bank information, birthday, and social security number.
- Do not share sexually explicit images or other materials.
- Do not engage with sexually explicit material online that includes people under age 18 years of age.

Pornography is ubiquitous online. It can be difficult to avoid, even for people who aren't trying to find it. That makes it almost a given that a young person will likely encounter pornography in their excursions around the web.

In an interview with SPARK for Autism, Eileen Crehan of Tufts says porn is very likely already on the radar of children who spend a lot of time online. This issue is a big one. Risks relate to consent versus coercion of the people in the images and video, malware and other threats when accessing certain sites, and inability to confirm age.

These are not comfortable discussions for a lot of parents, but they are important. Expert advice for parents applies to parents of autistic children, too. Because the complexity is greater than this chapter can encompass, I have provided a link to a resource from Common Sense Media at the end of the book.

Gender Identity and Sexual Orientation

The vast majority of education in the United States related to sex and relationships focuses on heterosexual perspectives and experiences of cisgender people. (Cisgender refers to someone whose gender expression aligns with their sex assigned at birth; Crehan et al., 2023). Autistic people are more likely to identify outside these experiences, including as transgender and gender diverse (Young & Cocallis, 2023). Even where education programs are available, the content may not be especially relatable. Research shows that autistic people are far more likely than nonautistic people to want information about gender identity and sexual orientation. This need can be met if education programs use scenarios with lesbian, gay, bisexual, transgender, queer, intersex, asexual, and others (LGBTQIA+) characters and situations.

Health and risk considerations vary with gender identity and orientation. As mentioned earlier in this chapter, for example, identifying as a member of the LGBTQIA+ community adds to the victimization risk for autistic people. Hence, aspects of risk, boundaries, and consent should be considered through the perspective of people who identify as LGBTQIA+. It is also important that the curriculum does not endorse homophobia, transphobia, or other marginalization, including with regard to race or class (Crehan et al., 2023).

There is some perception, which is reflected in some news coverage, that identifying as LGBTQIA+ is not genuine but instead is motivated by a desire to follow a trend. Evidence does not support this assumption. In a large study of more than 600,000 people (Warrier et al., 2020), most surveyed well before the current negative attention to the LGBTQIA+ population, 5% of people who were cisgender had autism. By comparison, 24% of those who identified as gender diverse had autism. Other evidence indicates that autistic girls are more likely to identify outside the gender role society assigns them (Brunissen et al., 2021).

Legislation in some states has focused on creating obstacles to gender-affirming care for autistic people. The argument is that they are not equipped to understand what is going on. This is infantilization and marginalization. Studies have shown that autistic people do understand their sexuality and sexual needs and strongly desire accurate and appropriate information about both.

As noted previously, sexuality and gender identity are key parts of every person's life. Someone who is assigned female at birth and identifies as a girl or woman instinctively understands that identity. Likewise, someone who is trans or nonbinary also has an instinctive understanding of their gender. This awareness can dawn as early as age 18 months, studies show, and becomes increasingly established with age, especially by the onset of puberty (George & Stokes, 2018). Anatomy at birth does not predict it and can sometimes include the coexistence of anatomy categorized both as male and as female.

People with anatomy and sex assigned at birth that diverge from the gender they experience have what is called *gender dysphoria*. The best way to address this unsettling feeling is to affirm the person's stated gender identity.

Evidence overwhelmingly shows that gender affirmation is best for mental health and other outcomes. Expert societies across all clinical specialties relevant to gender-affirming care for young people are in agreement that it saves lives and is evidence based.

What gender affirmation looks like highly depends on the child's age. For young prepubertal children, it consists mostly of verbal agreement, using the pronouns requested, and providing the desired clothing and haircuts, honoring autonomy. As discussed in the puberty chapter, for young people reaching puberty or their teens, hormonal interventions are possible. These include hormonal birth control that can suppress or limit menstruation and hormone blockers that can inhibit puberty-related development.

These interventions are not begun until puberty and can be stopped at any time. The vast majority of surgical interventions for gender affirmation are not available to people under age 18 in the United States. An exception is chest surgery, which can be performed after age 16 and following several years of medical therapy.

It is also important to know that there is substantial overlap between having autism and identifying as asexual or aromantic. Autistic people are more likely than nonautistic people to identify as asexual and/or aromantic (George & Stokes, 2018). These expressions of sexuality are widely misunderstood. People who are unfamiliar with them take them to imply no interest in sex, no history of having had sex, or simply an avoidance tactic because of fear of sex. None of these is accurate.

Asexual describes people who tend not to feel sexual desire for other people (Bush et al., 2021). That doesn't mean that they lack sexual desire in general or that they don't or won't have sex. Asexuality is a spectrum, however, and it's not all or nothing. Some terms on the asexuality spectrum include gray asexual (rare experiences of sexual desire) and demisexual (desire is experienced only when there is a deep connection to the other person). *Aromantic* simply means that the person experiences little or no romantic attraction to other people.

Masturbation

Masturbation is healthy and normal, and genital stimulation is a behavior that begins in utero (Gerhardt & Gravino, 2018). There should be no shame involved in talking about masturbation with your child, but establishing boundaries related to what is OK in private versus public are crucial.

Among autistic people, masturbation may be the most common sexual behavior, with 95% of those of male sex reporting the practice (Pecora et al., 2020). The rates are not especially different from those of nonautistic people. This practice is something that is developmentally appropriate and to be expected.

The conversations around masturbation will also be similar in many ways, regardless of neurobiology. They can include a discussion of which times of day are best for privacy (bedtime, shower time) and which places offer the most privacy. As I mentioned, sometimes young people use items that typically are not sex related to masturbate. It is important to be alert to tissue or other damage and to provide items that serve a similar purpose without harm.

Sidebar: Important Takeaways

- It's *my* body, mind, and life, and I get to decide what is right for *me*.
- It is OK to ask questions about sexuality and relationships.

> - Learning about sexuality helps me make healthy decisions in my life.
> - Everyone is a sexual being, including me.
> - I deserve to be in a healthy relationship. (based on McLaughlin, 2023)

Having Sex

Sex can and should be a healthy, fun part of life for those who have an interest in it. It can also be a stress reliever and anxiety reducer, which could be especially useful for autistic people.

Autistic people have sexual experiences that are similar to those of their nonautistic peers in terms of age at first encounter and other factors (Mhatre, 2021; Crehan et al., 2023; Dewinter et al., 2017). Findings are mixed, however. Some researchers suggest a slightly older age at the first encounter and less sexual activity with a partner among autistic people (Pecora et al., 2020).

There are boundaries to establish with a potential sexual or romantic partner. These include those already discussed, especially involving consent. Candid and direct communication styles are likely the best. Planning cues and discussing what is OK ahead of time may be a good idea because in-the-moment feelings can become overwhelming.

Every family has its own set of values. Every person also has their own set of beliefs and standards they set for themselves. A discussion of these values, what they look like, and how they might relate to sexuality and sex behaviors can help an autistic person clarify in advance what they'd like to do. Going through scenarios can be a good approach to deciding what these boundaries are and how to maintain them. Values change and can be age dependent, so revisiting this framing from time to time may be useful and enlightening.

Another boundary to bring up is when it is appropriate to talk about sex around other people—with rules to use as a guide. This kind of talk is usually quite personal and thus should be reserved for private times. Making clear what "private" looks like also is important: being alone, where no one but a partner can hear what is being talked about. In addition, these conversations are private between the partners and should not be shared with others.

Close friends may be good confidants to turn to with concerns or worries, if the friends show that they are comfortable with such conversations. Autistic people can get clarification around interpreting unclear cues from a partner, for example. In general, when in doubt, checking on who can hear the conversation and whose privacy needs to be protected can be a helpful guide about where the boundary lies.

Sidebar: Sensory Considerations

One possibly autistic-specific aspect of sexuality that receives little attention in even the most comprehensive sexuality education curricula is the role of sensory sensitivities. Sex behaviors, from kissing to intercourse, involve sounds, smells, and touch that may be uncomfortable or even overwhelming for an autistic person. Another facet of boundary setting that autistic people need to know about is respect for the need to take things slowly, make adjustments to the activity, stop completely, or discuss alternatives. It is OK to speak up when experiencing discomfort of any kind and ask for change.

Chapter Eight

Transition From High School

Every parent whose teen is inching—or speeding, depending on how time flies—toward adulthood has similar worries: What will my child do when they leave the comparatively regularly scheduled world of school and enter the "real" world? What will they need? How much will they need me? Where will the line be between facilitating and enabling or "oversupporting" in ways that limit acquisition of independence and necessary skills?

There is no single answer to these questions. But there are insights that may be useful as you and your teen begin to answer them. First, adolescence is a stage that can last into the mid-20s. This means that the supports a young adult needs can change as they transit through their 20s. What your family decides now should be flexible and adjustable as maturity and age support greater independence and responsibility.

Second, adulthood is a long time. As any adult can attest, it also is a process of continually learning from experience, meeting new people, and developing a support network that is independent of your family. One aim of the transition into adulthood is learning how to build this network so that when the inevitable happens—parents are no longer available—there's still that network of friends and supporters.

As many readers will acknowledge, our best-laid plans can always go sideways. Life has a way of derailing them. So although this chapter discusses planning a great deal, these plans should be viewed as maps in a largely uncharted territory. There will be some routes and obstacles to fill in or adjust as your child makes their way. As one parent told us, "As far as real life goes, once we were in it, it didn't matter how prepared we were on paper . . . I felt as unprepared as I did the day my children were born."

Despite the potential for derailment, plans are crucial for this huge transition from the (relatively) predictable, scheduled day-to-day world of childhood to the sometimes wildly unpredictable world of adults. The ideal for any child is that preparation has been a work in progress their entire lives, as they learn important skills for successful daily living and interacting with other people.

Throughout that time, even if the child's wishes were heard and considered, the adults were in charge of their days, their plans, and their lives. In adulthood, things will be different. For any teen, the aim in the transition to adulthood is to be able to take as much control of their lives as possible, whether bit by bit, all at once, or somewhere in between. That means making plans. In large part, these plans revolve around five areas that form the themes of this chapter on transition:

- deciding what to do after high school, whether that is work, training, or more schooling
- gaining and maintaining maximum independence in a safe and healthy way

- building support networks
- anticipating the "services cliff" and ensuring continued access to care and support
- being aware of relevant laws and other legal aspects

Several key terms will come up again and again in this chapter: self-determination, self-advocacy, and in(ter)dependence. Although I will elaborate much more on these concepts, briefly, self-determination is making one's own decisions about one's wants and needs, whereas self-advocacy is communicating those needs. In(ter)dependence relates to living an independent life while acting on the reality that no human is an island; even as we become independent in the sense of taking control over our lives and decisions, we also depend on each other (Organization for Autism Research [OAR], 2021).

Two other concepts to keep in mind as you and your teen plan for the transition to adulthood are *choice* and *opportunity*. These plans should offer options and openings for different experiences, with an eye to personal fulfillment, good quality of life, and control (as much as any of us have) over important aspects of daily life.

Self-Determination

Self-determination is defined as making your own choices about how you live your life (Malone, 2016; OAR, 2021). It's the flexibility that having options and choices gives us, so that we can select what feels and seems best for us in that moment. To quote the Autistic Self-Advocacy Network (ASAN), which provides ample and detailed transition materials and is listed in the resources at the end of this book, "Self-determination means that the final choices you make come from you." It is, ASAN says, the first step to becoming a self-advocate.

Self-Advocacy

Self-advocacy is communicating what we decided and working to get it. An important facet of becoming independent is this ability to self-advocate, or find ways to let people know what you need (Malone, 2016). Self-advocacy can be tough, especially in the face of daunting entities such as government organizations, medical establishments, employers, and schools. Regardless of their neurology, people can find themselves struggling to communicate their needs if they feel anxious or fearful about potential outcomes.

But it's important for a young person to learn how to communicate what they need. That can mean letting someone know when something is wrong, asking for help or support, or ensuring respect for and attention to their rights. I've talked about encouraging and supporting these practices in earlier chapters of the book. In a continuation of these practices, a large part of a transition plan will include working with the young person to recognize situations that require self-advocacy and practicing how to enact it.

Some Laws Relevant to Transition From High School

Before proceeding to specific aspects of transition, let's dive first into the alphabet soup of laws that are relevant to transitioning to adulthood. Some of these terms will be familiar to any family who has navigated establishing an Individualized

Education Program (IEP) for an autistic student. I discussed IEPs, including in the context of transition, in the chapter on schools (Chapter two).

In addition to IEPs, which feature in transition planning, families will need to be familiar with the Individuals With Disabilities Education Act (IDEA), Section 504 of the Rehabilitation Act of 1973 (commonly known as Section 504), and the American With Disabilities Act (ADA). Other abbreviations and acronyms that come into play in planning for and undergoing the transition to adulthood are the Affordable Care Act (ACA), the Health Insurance Portability and Accountability Act (HIPAA), and the Federal Education Right to Privacy Act (FERPA). Here is a brief bulleted summary of the relevance of each act:

- ACA—A healthcare reform law that, among other effects, originally required that all adults have health insurance. Since 2019, that has not been a federal requirement, but some states have established that requirement at the risk of tax penalties.
- ADA—A civil rights law that prohibits discrimination on the basis of disability, offering protection against such discrimination at school, in the workplace, and for receipt of public services. It requires reasonable accommodations for performing the essential functions of the person's role and for equal pay for disabled people.
- FERPA—This law protects the rights of students regarding provision to others of information about their school records and related information, among other elements. Up to age 18 or attendance at school beyond high school, parents have the right of review. A student who reaches eligibility (age 18 and/or attending a post–high school institution) takes over the right of access from their

parents but can grant a waiver for parents to also have access. In some special cases, parents can gain access without such a waiver, such as in a health or safety emergency or if they claim the student as a dependent on their taxes.
- HIPAA—A health privacy law that in part prevents healthcare entities from disclosing protected health information to someone other than the patient without that patient's consent.
- IDEA—An education law that guarantees free and appropriate education in the least restrictive environment to disabled students ages 3 to 21; its protections terminate for those over age 21.
- IEP—Under federal law (IDEA), a plan for transition must be part of the IEP by the time an autistic student reaches age 16 (so planning begins before this age), addressing (a) age-appropriate transition assessments, (b) measurable postsecondary goals, (c) transition services, and (d) courses of study (Malone, 2016). The IEP should begin to include a statement of transition service needs by the time the student is age 14, usually the age of entry into high school. A student with an IEP has the right to participate in their IEP meetings as a self-advocate. They also have the right to be included in meetings that involve transition planning and setting of postsecondary goals (Malone, 2016).
- Section 504—This civil rights law is intended to prevent discrimination against people with disabilities and applies to institutions that receive federal funding. An accommodations plan developed under this part of the law is called a *504 plan*. I touched on Section 504 in the chapter on schools.

Service Agencies

Every state has a department of education, and each of those departments has a special education agency. These organizations offer specifics about what the state requires for transition planning. The U.S. Department of Education maintains a links database where you can search for the proper agency for your state or region (https://www2.ed.gov/about/contacts/state/index.html).

Each state also has its own division of vocational rehabilitation, with some metropolitan areas also having local offices. The purpose of these vocational programs is to support job seeking for people with disabilities. In some states they are oversubscribed, with long waitlists. To find yours, you can search online for "division of vocational rehabilitation" and the name of your state, region, or territory. These services may also be offered within state departments of rehabilitation services. You also can search at this site for your state's agency (https://askearn.org/page/state-vocational-rehabilitation-agencies).

The federal government has an Administration on Disabilities that works at the state and local levels to support options and choices for people with disabilities to live with self-determination in their communities. It consists of three offices, the Office of Independent Living Programs, the Office of Intellectual and Developmental Disability, and the Office of Disability Services Innovation. Each of these has a specific brief with regard to supporting independent living, employment, and services for people with disabilities. More information is available on the government website (https://acl.gov/about-acl/administration-disabilities).

There also are state-level agencies under this umbrella that offer services related to transition planning, among others, for people with developmental disabilities. These agencies are responsible for offering post–high school education, training, and support. Their names vary somewhat, so to find your state's relevant agency, search here: https://www.nasddds.org/state-agencies/.

For information about Social Security Disability Insurance and Supplemental Security Income programs (respectively better known as SSDI and SSI), the federal government's website is https://www.ssa.gov/benefits/disability/. The red tape around accessing these services is notoriously tangled, but they are intended for people with high-support needs. SSDI is for people who are disabled and who have previously worked and paid Social Security taxes. SSI is intended for people with a disability who are on a limited income.

Many organizations have state or regional chapters or centers that work specifically with autistic people in accessing services and support. The U.S. Interagency Autism Coordinating Committee (https://iacc.hhs.gov/resources/organizations/private/) maintains a comprehensive list of private and nonprofit disability agencies and organizations that can serve as a starting point for finding resources in your area.

A note: If you have not been meticulously documenting every meeting and encounter related to your child's supports and other services, now is the time to begin doing so, including names, dates, what was discussed, instructions received, and any other information. Many families find themselves stuck in a loop of requests for documentation as they seek services for a family member with a disability.

Be complete, thorough, and organized and keep copies of everything. If you are missing copies of documentation, start making requests for them now. Parents of autistic teens who are making the transition to adulthood have many stories of spending hours, days, or weeks pulling together information after having been denied services for a child with high-support needs, even though the family provided abundant documentation going back to the preschool years.

Preparations and Planning

You and your child should begin a transition portfolio to maintain notes, files, and plans. The portfolio can be sectioned in any way that best suits you. Some possible sections include planning for daily life after high school, taking on activities of daily living, supports that might be needed, employment, estate planning, schooling or training, medical, financial, goals, housing, transportation, and resources. You also can keep records relevant to transition planning in this portfolio.

At the end of this book is a link to ASAN's transition guidance document, which includes recommendations for developing a transition notebook, complete with worksheets and detailed, plain-language guidance.

Briefly, ASAN recommends using a notebook with tabs for the sections you select. Their suggested tabs are personal information, education, career, community/independent living, adult services agencies, communication/social interaction, recreation and leisure, and other. But each individual will have categories that best suit their needs and planning processes.

Developing this portfolio and organizing sections can be one way for an autistic teen to express self-determination and begin making choices from the options available to them. I also provide a URL for the OAR's *A Guide for*

Transition to Adulthood, which similarly offers guidance, along with handouts and activities to use in shaping a transition plan.

I've already noted that for individuals who have IEPs, the law requires planning to be in place by the time the student turns 16. For transition-related goals within an IEP and in general, the aim is for them to be SMART, which stands for specific, measurable, achievable, relevant, and time-bound. Applying these features can keep goals concrete and doable, which can help prevent feeling overwhelmed or unsure. But what does that look like, and how does the student develop their goals? Here is an example:

> In considering what to do after graduating from high school, Alyssa, working with her parents, teachers, and close friend, made a list of things she enjoys. Her favorite activities are being outside and working with plants. She especially likes taking care of plants and making sure that they are healthy. Her favorites are the plants that grow flowers.
>
> An aim that arises from Alyssa's enjoyment of these activities could be related to working at a plant nursery. But simply writing down "Alyssa will get a job at a plant nursery" does not meet the elements of setting a SMART goal. Many elements are missing.
>
> Alyssa's school requires seniors to engage in a community service project during their senior year. Here is an opportunity to check several boxes at once for Alyssa while setting a SMART transition-related goal: "In the spring of her junior year, Alyssa will work with the community service project coordinator to identify local volunteer opportunities that involve planting flowers or

trees and/or caring for flowers or trees. She will volunteer for an opportunity that fits her school schedule and transportation needs, committing to at least 4 hours a month through the summer. This participation will support her accrual of community service hours through a personal interest and her exploration of horticulture as a potential career path."

The goal is specific (identify volunteer opportunities, with support from an experienced adult), measurable (find one opportunity, commit to up to 4 hours a month), achievable (greening campaigns/school or organizational planting for nonprofits/community gardens/local parks and recreation, etc., are often in search of volunteers, with minimal hours requirements), relevant (she will gain valid experience in an area of interest, possibly make connections with people who could become part of a network, and work toward meeting a senior community service requirement), and time-bound (through the summer).

In addition, it starts small, with a few volunteer hours a month, rather than, say, seeking full-time employment at a local plant nursery and committing to a full summer at 40 hours a week. Often, it's best for an autistic adolescent to start in increments to get used to something new in small bouts, rather than taking bigger leaps (Eagle, 2021), but as always, the right choice will be specific to the person and the family.

A transition plan can include goals in several categories, including education, independent living, and employment. In developing these goals, the student and their family can consider likes and dislikes, interests, current competencies, future aspirations, and logistics related to housing and transportation. Several transition-specific assessment tools are available for families to use in writing up their plan and making decisions about goals. I've included web addresses for some resources at the end of the book.

All planning for adulthood should respect the young person's need for self-determination and always include their input, using whatever communication tools they rely on to be understood. This centering of the person (OAR, 2021) also supports a key piece of transition planning: that the aims and goals take into account and leverage the interests and inclinations of the young person. The previous example about Alyssa illustrates how this might look. This approach echoes similar tactics for promoting social engagement and connection discussed in previous chapters. Including the student in every step of this process also better equips them with the tools they need to self-advocate—to make their self-determined wishes known—outside structured settings and without supports they may have had from parents and other adults.

In fact, learning or practicing these skills in self-determination and self-advocacy can be among the transition plan goals. They also should be a part of every IEP meeting, if your child has an IEP, in an authentic and meaningful way. Meeting attendees should address the student directly. The student should be given space to participate in the meeting in the role that's most comfortable for them, whether they are leading it or spending most of it as an observer. A major aim of transition planning is to equip the autistic person with skills in self-determination and self-advocacy. These meetings themselves offer (one hopes) a safe place to practice them effectively.

The Parent Role

> "Of course, I'm worried about the future for my sons—that's why [I] tried to put into place everything [I] can to . . . give our sons the best education and support to help them both become as independent as they possibly can."
>
> —A parent of two autistic sons

This parent's comments get to the heart of what every parent wants for their child, autistic or not: to have the tools they need to function independently and well in life. But it can be hard to take a step back after years and years of advocating and fighting for your child and what they need for success. And it's even harder to loosen the grip of anxiety about what will happen to an adult child with high-support needs, especially once parents are no longer there.

Both situations have the same solution: Do as much as possible for your child to lay the groundwork for self-determination, self-advocacy, and a support network. The translation is that, yes, parents will have to take a step back into an advisory role in many cases and let their child take some risks and learn from experiences, which can be the best learning tool.

While the teen is still in high school, though, there's plenty parents can be doing for transition planning in their ongoing role of parenting a child. In many or most cases, no one will know the child better than the parents do. Parents can at least initially take the lead in working with the student to develop lists of future goals and foresee challenges and obstacles. OAR suggests that parents envision what they'd like their child's life to look like in increments of 5, 10, or 20 years out and begin working on a plan of steps to achieve those outcomes (and avoid unwanted outcomes; OAR, 2021).

These goals should be aspirational and contain elements of challenge, risk, and room for the young autistic adult to grow and gain independence skills. The plan should acknowledge gaps or mitigation steps that might be needed to achieve these goals and include plans for them. It's also good to be creative about the young person's skills and traits and to consider different perspectives when evaluating where the autistic teen's strengths lie. For example, if the young person does best when adhering to a fixed schedule, that can be a strength in pursuits that require highly rigorous observance of schedules. In turn, it can be incorporated into considerations of possible post–high school pursuits.

Finally, in developing goals, don't neglect less quantifiable aspects of a good quality of life that may be important to your autistic child, such as "spending time outdoors" or "going to a movie on Saturday." Consider what they enjoy and what tools they'll need to continue their enjoyments as adults.

This entire process may be frustrating for several reasons. Your adolescent may not want your help, as can be the way of young people taking their first steps toward adulthood and newly expanded independence. Your contribution to the work and the work itself may be proportionally different from what you see other parents in this situation doing. You may even know parents of autistic adolescents who aren't doing this at all. These frustrations are completely understandable and are shared by many parents! It might help at the most trying moments to remind yourself that if you don't get it taken care of, no one else will.

The other role for parents in transition planning is one that many parents of autistic children know well: Advocate for your child when they can't, with an eye to equipping them to be able to do so. As the adults, parents should also monitor the

IEP (as they likely have been), if the child has one, to ensure progress on its aims and implementation. As most parents of autistic children would agree, keeping tabs on these elements is key to faithfully following the IEP.

As part of transition, however, parents can support their autistic child in monitoring progress and implementation themselves and in communicating concerns when issues arise. The IEP team should be working closely with both the student and their parents in developing and implementing the transition plan, including how to coordinate with public services (transportation, vocational, etc.) where relevant.

Parents can engage in an ongoing conversation with their teens about their plans after high school, walking them through what their aims might entail. For example, if the teen would like to take college classes, parents can talk to them about different options, from online to community college to in-person enrollment at a university. I've written in previous chapters about guiding autistic teens through independence in their activities of daily living. But these final years of K–12 school are a time to emphasize establishing good hygiene and other habits. If your autistic child eventually attends a postsecondary institution, if they can live at home in the meantime, doing so stretches out the time for practicing these habits with your support.

The watchword of this march to transition, however, is *empowerment*. The usual advice for raising an adolescent applies for autistic adolescents as well: Like any teens, they need room to take risks (within reason), room to fail, and room to learn from these experiences. And they still need parents to help process what they're going through, help them evaluate what's happening, and reflect on lessons and learnings. The level of risk, the amount of room, the kind of processing, and the reflection will all vary from family to family. But the role of the parent will be an almost paradoxical duality of offering a safe harbor while encouraging independence.

Planning Tools

All of this planning can seem overwhelming, even to people with the most well-honed organizational skills. The good news is that no one needs to reinvent the wheel because tools are available to support this process.

I've already mentioned the ASAN and OAR guides. Parents and their autistic students can use them to brainstorm, make lists, and develop a transition plan that respects self-determination, reflects the autistic student's interests, and incorporates reasonable risks within SMART goals. In addition, there are person-centered planning tools that transition teams can use: Making Action Plans and Planning Alternative Tomorrows With Hope. I have provided links to information about these tools in the resources list at the end of the book.

The Planning Team and The Plan

The transition planning team can vary in its makeup. In addition to your autistic child and you, the team may include other interested family members, a transition coordinator, teachers, therapists (psychologist, speech language pathologist, occupational therapist), and administrators. Other potential team members could include guidance counselors, a specialized advocate, and representatives from services agencies. Autistic peers also can be key contributors to such a team (Capozzi et al., 2019).

The Services Cliff

The services cliff for people with disabilities who age out of pediatric medical care is notorious. One day, the child is age 17 years and 364 days and can still visit their pediatric specialists. The next day, they are no longer eligible and must find new, adult specialists. The same cliff exists for other services. Of all the things that parents and their children must plan for in the adult transition for a teen who has a disability, this approaching cliff is among the most significant.

When a teen ages out of medical care or the school system, the sudden end of services for "children" represents the cliff that awaits. The medical care piece may be the most difficult and may seem almost impossible to navigate. As one parent of an autistic child who had a medically complex disability told me when she sought care for her son during this time, she was told, "I don't see patients over 17, and the current waitlist is 2 years." She concluded that it would be wise to start planning for this approaching cliff at least 2 years out.

Another parent described having spent 4 months trying to get an adult consult at a major tertiary care center in their area as their child approached the end of pediatric care. They learned that the pattern of care for adults was far different: Specialists were more siloed from each other than in the pediatric setting. That meant much more work to ensure continuity of care on several medical fronts for their child. Additionally noting that they learned that self-referral is not possible for adult care, this parent said, "It's a perfect storm."

Parents can also feel that the pediatric specialists "tried harder" with "doors open wide." "I hid in pediatrics too long," one told us, adding, "I should have thought about just how many things I'd be transitioning at one time." As the many headings in this chapter on transition imply, this transitional period covers every aspect of life, from medical to daily living to education and employment to housing. "The whole 'adult' transition is pretty gut wrenching," said one parent.

I do not mean to frighten parents with this information. Rather, I want to emphasize that beginning preparations years before the transition period arrives is wise, in part because there is so much to do. If you give your family this space of time for preparation and work through each aspect of transition planning (using notebooks and lists provided by advocacy groups and others, for example), the process will feel—and be—more manageable. By the time your child reaches the cliff, perhaps you'll have constructed a sturdy safety net for them.

Guardianship

One especially difficult decision for families to make centers on guardianship. In this formal, legal situation, someone takes parental-level responsibility for an autistic adult and has the final say in all decisions about their lives (ASAN, 2017). This measure could be viewed as sitting at the far end on the spectrum of independence, lying at the greatest distance from the primary goals of transition preparation and entry into adulthood, which are to support, to the greatest possible extent, self-determination, self-advocacy, and independence in choosing among their options.

States have their own laws regarding guardianships. You can find the pertinent information for your state on the website for the National Resource Center for Supported Decision-Making (https://supporteddecisionmaking.org/). As the name implies, this organization works toward the other end of the spectrum of support for adults who have disabilities, with an approach known as supported decision-making. A well-intended guardian could, of course, still make space for these features and for supported decision-making. As with many other decisions that must be made around this transition period, building in as much flexibility as possible with an eye to a balance between risk and safety will be a highly personal process.

Supported Decision-Making

The concept of supported decision-making relies on a support team for the autistic person. The team should consist of people with expertise or close personal knowledge of the person, those whom they can trust for advice and support. In other words, as the National Resource Center for Supported Decision-Making says, it "is just a fancy way of describing how we all make choices." We all turn to people who have the right understanding of either the situation (medicine, housing, taxes) or ourselves to aid us in making a decision.

What's key is that the support team consists of people whom the autistic person can trust. Knowing that this group of people exists can reduce anxiety and make space for the autistic person to think clearly and carefully and exercise self-determination in making choices. They can also engage in self-advocacy with people they trust and are comfortable enough with to be candid.

As noted previously, it's possible for a guardian within a guardianship to operate through the supported decision-making model. But the legality of the situation is that with a guardianship, the guardian will always have the final say. Building and working with a support team for supported decision-making is a lifetime practice of "interdependence," acknowledging that we never spend any time of our lives as an island. As ASAN notes in its transition planning materials, "Supported decision-making is for anyone," of any age (Malone, 2016).

Legal Planning

I am not trained in law and I encourage readers to consult with someone who has specific training around power of attorney, representative payees, estate planning, special needs trusts, and other aspects specific to special needs and/or disabilities. There are attorneys who specialize in these services.

In *A Guide for Transition to Adulthood*, available at https://researchautism.org/resources/a-guide-for-transition-to-adulthood/, OAR offers some advice around legal planning, including creating a will, a special needs trust, and what is called an "ABLE" account, which is a tax-advantaged savings accounts for people with disabilities and their families (OAR, 2021). This planning requires the meticulous attention of an attorney. Even what seem to be basic decisions, such as a will that leaves everything to your autistic child, can leave them ineligible to continue receiving some services.

Housing

Housing decisions for a young autistic adult will take a host of factors into account. These factors include their plans after high school (work, school, both, neither), their inclinations and their family's, space availability, housing costs in the area, daily support needs, and personal preferences regarding shared facilities versus living alone. Students who attend college or university and plan to live in a dorm can look into housing reserved for students whose disability calls for them to live in a single-occupancy room, if that's their preference.

Some states have "shared-living" programs that your family can search for online. These programs connect people who may need support and can involve paid staff or other arrangements for mutual support. Cooperative living, or "co-ops," which often revolve around a shared interest and shared responsibilities, are another option.

Keep in mind that the arc of development will continue for young autistic adults. As they gain age and experience, initial housing decisions and desires may change. Note that the Fair Housing Act makes it illegal for a landlord to engage in discrimination against a potential tenant because of a disability and must allow for reasonable accommodations.

Another category of housing to consider is a center for independent living. These centers exist specifically for people with disabilities, who also run them, and they provide services that support independence. You can learn more about these centers and find out about those in your state at the U.S. Administration for Community Living website (https://acl.gov/programs/aging-and-disability-networks/centers-independent-living). OAR warns that waitlists for these programs can be long.

Note that, thanks to the Supreme Court's decision in the 1999 *Olmstead v. L.C.* case, people with disabilities have the right to live in their communities in the most integrated setting. You can learn more about *Olmstead* at the U.S. Department of Health and Human Services website (https://www.hhs.gov/civil-rights/for-individuals/special-topics/community-living-and-olmstead/index.html). Briefly, states are tasked with providing services within the community (rather than in an institution) for people with disabilities who otherwise would be eligible for institutional services. Three conditions must be met: The placement is appropriate, the person agrees with the placement, and the placement "can be reasonably accommodated" with regard to the state's available resources and the needs of the rest of the population with disability. The law helps people with disabilities avoid institutionalization. The services are accessible through Medicaid programs.

Families can work with their autistic teen to prepare for the maximum independence in housing by supporting them toward independently engaging in activities of daily living, planning their days, planning and preparing meals, and maintaining their personal space (including laundry).

Employment

Research shows that autistic people experience immense obstacles when it comes to finding employment and staying employed. The system is struggle enough for people without disabilities. The challenges on all fronts can be magnified for an autistic person. Even when legal supports are in place, their application is fragmented and uneven.

As one parent of two autistic sons commented to me, their family tries to give their sons space to "explore and have fun" as young adults. On the employment front, however, their sons have been fired over a text message and ghosted by an employer (meaning the employer just stopped contacting them). In one case, the family turned to developing a Plan to Achieve Self-Support to use SSI to bridge the financial gap while their sons sought other employment. This government program is intended to support people with disabilities in returning to work if they receive SSI or could qualify for it (for more information about the Plan to Achieve Self-Support program, see the U.S. government's site at https://www.ssa.gov/disabilityresearch/wi/pass.htm).

In the end, whether an autistic person pursues postsecondary education, vocational training, a job, or some combination, employment is usually the ultimate aim. Jobs are important because they give a person a sense of purpose and support them in meeting their personal needs. But having a job as a person with a disability can be tricky to navigate. It requires making decisions, from disclosing a so-called hidden disability to self-advocating for the reasonable accommodations that the law requires employers to offer.

Employment falls into different categories (Malone, 2016), including the well-known competitive full-time versus part-time jobs, contract or self-employment (which can make tax filing more complex), supported employment, and vocational rehabilitation. Government employment programs that support people with disabilities in getting work include the U.S. Department of Labor's Employment First program (more information can be found online at https://www.dol.gov/agencies/odep/initiatives/employment-first) and Schedule A letters, which document the person's disability and give federal agencies the ability to hire a qualified person with a disability without putting the applicant through the long, complicated process of competitive hiring (you can find more on Schedule A letters at https://www.dol.gov/sites/dolgov/files/odep/wrp/scheduleachecklist.pdf). Supported employment is also government supported and usually involves working with a job coach through the state's vocational rehabilitation agency.

Support also can involve training and job development skills, but these factors vary by state. The jobs usually are competitive, so the autistic person would work alongside nonautistic people. Common job settings include universities, the service industry, and small businesses (OAR, 2021).

ASAN's *Roadmap to Transition: A Handbook for Autistic Youth Transitioning to Adulthood* (https://autisticadvocacy.org/book/roadmap/) contains guidance, details, and planning documents that may serve as a good starting point for exploring the various options. The Center on Secondary Education for Students With Autism Spectrum Disorders also offers a series of informational seminars and publications that might be useful (more information is available at https://csesa.fpg.unc.edu/professionals/supporting-transition), as does OAR's *A Guide for Transition to Adulthood*.

During the planning process for transition while your child is still in high school, the formal or informal plan can include various activities oriented toward an employment future. These activities may include job shadowing (even virtual job shadowing), conducting informational interviews with people employed in an area of interest, and, as in the prior vignette about Alyssa, gaining experience through volunteering. It's also a good idea to practice how to deal with rejection because any job search will almost inevitably involve rejections. It is also common to never hear from a prospective employer at all, so practicing how to deal with radio silence after applying is important.

College

Consider the following story:

> After high school, an autistic student decided to defer their college acceptance for a year. During that time,

they lived at home, took a few community college classes, and regrouped following their K–12 experiences. When the student did matriculate and move into a dorm, their home base was about a half hour away. They had wanted that nearness so that there would be a supportive place to go that was not too close, but not too far away.

This route is not a conventional one to college. But autism can involve an atypical developmental trajectory, and shifting the time frame for any life milestone can be an important accommodation. In this case, the student's parents made way for their autistic teen to express self-determination and self-advocate for the yearlong delay of college. The autistic teen then lived independently, with the "safe" home base still close enough for comfort.

Contrast that with another parent's comment to us:

> We are taught how to advocate towards post-secondary education like it's a milestone [that's] not affected by a developmental *delay*. I felt so much emotional weight about getting my [child] to the next milestone even though I cognitively knew many of these things would happen in their own time if I just provided the support they needed and the opportunities to engage in all sorts of things.

These stories underscore the need for flexibility in transition planning and the need to, if possible, sketch out Plans A, B, and C—or more—in case things change.

If your child does attend college and needs supports, schools have a student disability services office that is responsible for planning and providing those supports. Academically, these accommodations can include extended time for tests, testing in a specific quiet environment, note-taking assistance, and assistive technologies.

The disability services office will require documentation of the disability before establishing a plan. The student can then share an accommodations letter with their instructors, who are expected to abide by the accommodations and respect the student's privacy. Instructors also are expected to include a statement about accommodations and disability services in their syllabus. Presenting these letters is one of many acts of self-advocacy that will be required for an autistic college student.

Not all postsecondary institutions are the same. Those that are called colleges tend to be 4-year institutions that focus on bachelor's degrees. Private colleges tend to be smaller, so a student can perhaps be better "seen" and attended to, but they can also be quite expensive. Universities are also 4-year institutions, but they additionally offer graduate degrees in many disciplines.

A community college is a local institution that offers 2-year or associate's degrees, often along with some 4-year programs. These schools tend to be more affordable and offer students the potential to live at home while attending classes. For those who prefer hands-on activities or who are anticipating employment in a skilled field, vocational schools or an apprenticeship might be the best choice for gaining the appropriate education.

Regardless of where the newly minted autistic adult lands, the venue will be new and possibly unsettling. The transition plan should also include a road map for managing the new situation, using the tools that the autistic person developed throughout high school. Finding acquaintances and making friends could be especially daunting. Seeking out campus clubs and activities that they enjoy is one entry point.

Money Management

For intricate financial planning related to support of an autistic child, families should consult with specialists who have expertise in this area. But an autistic teen should learn as much as they can about personal money management, a subject that tends to be overlooked for teenagers in general within formal education.

As with all other aspects of independence, experience and practice make the best teachers. An autistic teen should start by working with a basic budget and tracking their spending. Family members can offer feedback and guidance on how the tracking is going, where expenses exceed resources, and practices that can help keep a budget in balance.

There also are apps that track expenses in different categories, such as food, entertainment, and education, that the young person can use to keep tabs on their money and to get a feel for how much things cost.

Driving

Autistic people are often interested in learning to drive. A 2017 study found that one in three autistic adolescents will obtain at least a learner's permit, with more than 90% receiving their license within 2 years after that (Curry et al., 2018). Being able to drive can be an important skill because it facilitates self-determination and independence, including successful engagement in activities of daily living. That said, driving is not the only way to get from Point A to Point B, so the skill is useful but not necessarily indispensable.

Autistic teens might benefit from a longer time frame for practicing driving skills and getting comfortable with driving on their own. This practice can be especially important for autistic young people whose executive function or attentional issues might require more practice in focusing and avoiding distractions while driving. Some autistic young adults may not want to start driving until later adulthood. Their reasons can include anxiety about sequencing and the split-second judgment and decision-making driving requires or a reluctance to try something so new to them.

Wellness and Healthcare

Some states start phasing in access limitations from an earlier age, so it is advisable to check on your state's consent rules regarding a child's medical records and age cutoffs. One sometimes surprising event in a parent's life is the sudden realization that they cannot access the medical records of a child who has just turned 18. Electronic health record portals that are accessible to patients may now give warnings upon sign-in of an impending change in their child's status. Otherwise, parents have no hint. So be aware that at age 18, your child's medical right to privacy becomes their own, with some exceptions.

Another change with the turning of the calendar is the switch from pediatric to adult care. One way to prepare for this switch is to change from seeing a pediatrician for primary care to seeing a family practice doctor. Family practice doctors can provide continuity of care throughout the teen years and into adulthood. For specialty care, access will depend on many factors, including type of insurance, location and distance from specialty care centers, and waiting lists for adult specialists.

For the sake of independence, it's a good idea to begin shifting medical and wellness scheduling and practices over to your child to the greatest possible extent, under your guidance. If they can, have them call to make appointments, check in at a medical office on their own, fill or refill prescriptions, be the primary person speaking in the room during an appointment, have privacy according to their wishes during appointments, and set up and maintain online access to their health records.

Take opportunities as they arise for your child to take the wheel and to know about their own personal medical histories, including any allergies and medications they take (Izurieta, 2022). Their medical self-determination starts with being informed. That extends to an ongoing education in U.S. healthcare and the intricacies of health insurance, copays, and types of care (e.g., urgent versus emergency, primary versus specialty).

At home, they can participate in their wellness and medical care by learning how to schedule medications using an app or a pill box separated by day and time, as well as learning how to take their temperature and recognize other signs of illness. They also can create or purchase a first-aid kit of their own, with instructions for how each element in the kit is used. As part of this process, they should also learn and practice what to do in an emergency, including important phone numbers (doctor, parents, neighbors) and when to call 911.

Entering adulthood can mean undergoing new types of exams for young people. A gynecological exam especially can be scary and uncomfortable. But it's important for preventive care and, as addressed in the chapter on puberty, for other forms of care. Do what you can to find a clinician who is sensitive to common accommodations for people with disabilities, including autistic people. The clinician should be willing to be patient and take the time to explain everything that is happening.

It also may be helpful to walk the young person through the process of any medical exam to make it less surprising. For gynecological exams, some experts suggest practicing relaxation techniques beforehand or bringing along something that will serve as a distraction, such as a video game (Vanderbilt Kennedy Center, 2021b). Keep in mind that healthcare facilities must ensure effective communication to people with disabilities.

For autistic teens who identify as lesbian, gay, bisexual, transgender, queer, intersex, asexual, and others, some aspects of medical care may be inadequate to their needs, or they may not be heard or understood in expressing their gender identity. They may need aid from their support network in finding a practitioner who affirms their gender identity and provides care accordingly (Hall et al., 2020).

In Closing

It bears remembering that having autism doesn't mean "not developing." Autistic teens are on a developmental trajectory just like nonautistic teens are. Where they exist on that arc toward adulthood can change slowly or quickly and be "typical" or not typical. Where your teen is right now is likely to be different from where they are in a few months, and then it will change again. For this reason, although transition plans should be specific and concrete, they need to have flexibility and choices baked into them as well.

Glossary

Ableism Discrimination against people with disabilities.
Activities of daily living The activities of taking care of oneself, including personal hygiene, eating, bathing, and getting from place to place.
Adolescence The life phase of maturing from a child into an adult, behaviorally and otherwise.
Affordable Care Act (ACA) A healthcare reform law.
Americans With Disabilities Act (ADA) A civil rights law that prohibits discrimination on the basis of disability.
Anxiety A feeling of fear, dread, or uneasiness, and, if chronic, not in proportion to or related to specific triggers or threats.
Asexual A tendency not to feel sexual desire about other people.
Attention-deficit/hyperactivity disorder (ADHD) A neurodevelopmental condition characterized by impairments in attention and focus, sometimes with difficulties related to impulse control and hyperactivity.
Augmentative and alternative communication Methods that support, supplement, or replace speaking and/or writing.
Broad autism phenotype The presence of traits that resemble features of autism but do not meet the diagnostic criteria for having autism.
Camouflage In this context, efforts to "mask" behaviors associated with having autism.
Cisgender A status in which gender expression aligns with the sex assigned at birth.
Cognition The processes that support thinking, learning, and reasoning.
Cognitive behavioral therapy A kind of talk therapy that is focused on changing negative patterns of thought.

Connective tissue disorders Connective tissue refers to any of the tissue types that hold the body together, including bone, blood, and tendons and ligaments. These tissues consist in part of proteins that, in turn, are encoded in many different genes. Some variants of these genes result in proteins that function differently, often being more "stretchy" than normal, and possibly leading to various related conditions. One well-known group of connective tissue disorders falls under the Ehlers–Danlos category. Marfan syndrome is another well-known example.

Core features of autism The key traits that support a diagnosis of autism, including problems with social communication and interaction and restricted or repetitive behaviors or interests.

Cyberbullying Bullying carried out through the use of digital tools, such as social media platforms.

Demisexual Desire is experienced only when there is a deep connection to the other person.

Diagnostic and Statistical Manual of Mental Disorders This book, in its fifth edition with a subsequent text revision, is a compendium of the diagnostic criteria for various mental health–related and neurodevelopmental conditions, including autism.

Diagnostic overshadowing The presence of one diagnosis diverts attention from signs or symptoms of another condition or causes those signs and symptoms to be attributed to the known diagnosis.

Echolalia Repeating heard words or phrases.

Epilepsy A condition of experiencing recurrent seizures.

Expressive language Communication output, verbal or nonverbal, to express oneself to others.

Externalizing behavior Turning negative energy outward, for example, behaving aggressively.

Federal Education Right to Privacy Act (FERPA) Protects the rights of students regarding provision to others of information about their school records and related information.

Fragile X–related primary ovarian insufficiency (FXPOI) A condition that can arise in people with fragile X syndrome whose ovaries do not function at typical levels.

Fragile X syndrome (FXS) A genetic condition that traces to changes on the X chromosome and that is related developmental delay, learning disabilities, and social communication difficulties; often co-occurs with autism.

Free and appropriate education An expected guarantee for students with disabilities in public K–12 schools in the United States, documented in the child's Individualized Education Program.

Gastroesophageal reflux disease The condition of stomach acid surging upward into the esophagus, causing a burning feeling; common among autistic people.

Gender A socially defined role as a boy/man, girl/woman, nonbinary, or other category based on behavior, identity, and social factors that varies across time and cultures globally.

Gender diverse Gender identity and expression that are at variance with current gender norms and/or extends beyond the "man/woman, as assigned at birth" binary; also given as LGBTQIA+, which stands for lesbian, gay, bisexual, queer, transgender, intersex, asexual/aromantic, plus. The "plus" references many other genders that people express.

Gender identity A person's sense of their gender, regardless of sex assigned at birth.

Health Insurance Portability and Accountability Act (HIPAA) Health privacy law that in part precludes healthcare entities from disclosing protected health information to someone other than the patient without that patient's consent.

Hypermobility spectrum disorders Genetic disorders of the connective tissue that lead to highly mobile joints (commonly known as double-jointedness, for example), pain, joint instability, and heightened injury risk.

Individualized Education Program A written legal document detailing an education plan that meets the learning needs of a student with disabilities. It is intended to ensure that every child being educated in a public school receives a free and appropriate education in the least restrictive environment possible.

Individuals With Disabilities Education Act (IDEA) The law that enshrines the right to a free and appropriate education in the least restrictive environment possible for children with disabilities.

Intellectual disability A broad category that includes people who experience impairments in one or more aspects of intellectual functioning and ability to adapt behavior to different contexts; it is not part of an autism diagnosis but can co-occur with having autism.

Internalizing behavior Turning negative mental energy onto the self.

IQ Intelligence quotient, a number derived from performance on a battery of tests of cognition, designed to measure how a person performs relative to peers of the same age. The numbers derived from these tests are relative to other people, and a person's scores can change, especially during the first 2 or 3 decades of life.

Letterboards In this context, a printed or digital layout of the letters of the alphabet in order and, where relevant, of numbers. Users communicate by spelling out words by indicating the appropriate letters.

Least restrictive environment An element of the rights that the law requires be met for children with disabilities who are being educated in U.S. K–12 public schools, documented in the child's Individualized Education Program. The least restrictive environment that is possible is education within the general school population, in general education, as opposed to special education, classrooms.

Neurodevelopmental Related to brain development during the embryonic, fetal, or other developmental period.

Neurodiversity The range of behaviors and neurotypes that humans manifest, with an implicit element of acceptance and accommodation for all neurotypes.

Neurotypical Having a neurotype (brain/behavior) within typical patterns, without a developmental or other neurobiologically related condition or diagnosis.

Nocturnal enuresis Urinating at night during sleep.

Obsessive-compulsive disorder (OCD) A condition that involves experiencing uncontrollable, reoccurring thoughts and/or behaviors, with the urge to repeat them over and over.

Off-label Use of a prescription-only medication for a condition or indication other than those for which it was approved.

Oppositional defiant disorder A condition that features persistent, frequent defiance of and anger toward authority figures.

Plan to Achieve Self-Support A program intended to support people with disabilities in returning to work if they receive Supplemental Security Income or could qualify for it.

Prevalence A snapshot taken at a specific time of the proportion of people in the population who have a condition.

Proloquo2Go An augmentative and alternative communication app that offers a letterboard and images, along with a voice feature to support verbal communication.

Puberty The process of maturation of the organs related to reproduction.

Receptive language Understanding of information provided (received) verbally and nonverbally, visually, and otherwise.

Schedule A letter Documents the person's disability and gives federal agencies the ability to hire a qualified person who has a disability without putting the applicant through the long, complicated process of competitive hiring.

Section 504 A Part of the Rehabilitation Act of 1973 that prevents discrimination against students with disabilities who are participating in federally funded programs.

Self-advocacy Communicating one's needs and wants.

Self-determination Making one's own decisions and choices about what one wants and needs.

Self-injurious behavior (SIB) A term capturing a wide array of behaviors that can cause harm to the person, including head banging against objects and biting.

Sex In this context, a status assigned at birth based largely on external anatomy, which is identified as male, female, or intersex.

Social engineering In this context, the planning of social activities and interactions, such as "play dates."

Social thinking This term was coined by speech-language pathologist Michelle Garcia Winner, and it emphasizes social problem-solving, cognitive flexibility, and thinking about the emotions and points of view of others.

Social Security Disability Insurance (SSDI) An assistance program for those who qualify.

Supplemental Security Income (SSI) A federal assistance program for those who qualify.

Tuberous sclerosis complex (TSC) A genetic condition that leads to the growth of tuber-like, noncancerous tumors in the skin, kidney, heart, brain, and lungs. It is a relatively common co-occurring condition with autism.

Vesicoureteral reflux A condition in which urine backs up from the bladder, sometimes all the way to the kidneys.

Resources

Chapter One

- American Psychological Association, summary of the update to the *Diagnostic and Statistical Manual of Mental Disorders-5* (*DSM-5*) for the *DSM-5-TR*: https://www.psychiatry.org/File%20Library/Psychiatrists/Practice/DSM/DSM-5-TR/APA-DSM5TR-DiagnosesforChildren.pdf
- Center on Secondary Education for Students With Autism Spectrum Disorder, information on autism in girls: https://csesa.fpg.unc.edu/sites/csesa.fpg.unc.edu/files/resources/AAG-Autism%20in%20Females.pdf
- Hayden's story at the UK's National Autistic Society website: https://www.autism.org.uk/advice-and-guidance/stories/reuben-s-story
- Proloquo2Go AAC: This app is available through the Apple app store and can be used with iPad, iPhone, and Apple Watch: https://apps.apple.com/us/app/proloquo2go-aac/id308368164
- Stanford Neurodiversity Project, for more on neurodiversity: https://med.stanford.edu/neurodiversity.html
- U.S. Centers for Disease Control and Prevention: *DSM-5* diagnostic criteria for autism: https://www.cdc.gov/ncbddd/autism/hcp-dsm.html
- U.S. Interagency Autism Coordinating Committee: Diagnostic criteria for autism and for social (pragmatic) communication disorder, with tables for severity ratings: https://iacc.hhs.gov/about-iacc/subcommittees/resources/dsm5-diagnostic-criteria.shtml

Chapter Two

- Autistic Self Advocacy Network: Their collection of school-related resources is at https://autisticadvocacy.org/actioncenter/issues/school/
- Center for Parent Information & Resources: Their database of state-based information parent training centers is at https://www.parentcenterhub.org/find-your-center/.
- The Center on Secondary Education for Students with Autism Spectrum Disorder maintains many resources, including *Understanding Autism: A Guide for Secondary School Teachers*, at https://csesa.fpg.unc.edu/resources/understanding-autism-guide-secondary-school-teachers.
- Individualized Education Programs and 504 plans: A comparison of the two (in the context of attention-deficit/hyperactivity disorder) is in *ADDitude* magazine, available at https://www.additudemag.com/iep-vs-504-plan-idea-adhd-disability-education/, and another comparison is at the University of Washington's website at https://www.washington.edu/accesscomputing/what-difference-between-iep-and-504-plan.
- TIES Center, which offers tools for ensuring the most inclusive (least restrictive) environment for students with disabilities: https://tiescenter.org/
- U.S. Department of Education: An example of an Individualized Education Program form: https://www2.ed.gov/policy/speced/guid/idea/modelform-iep.pdf
- U.S. Department of Education, Office of Civil Rights: Information about how to file a discrimination complaint is available at https://www2.ed.gov/about/offices/list/ocr/docs/howto.html.
- Wrightslaw, an indispensable source for families navigating the disability-related legal landscape: https://www.wrightslaw.com/info/advo.index.htm

Chapter Three

- Ehlers–Danlos Society: Information about Ehlers–Danlos syndrome, including signs and symptoms and an inventory of known genetic variants, available at https://www.ehlers-danlos.com/what-is-eds/
- Epilepsy Foundation: Information about autism and epilepsy at https://www.epilepsy.com/stories/epilepsy-and-autism-there-relationship
- National Fragile X Foundation: This organization offers information about fragile X syndrome and autism at https://fragilex.org/understanding-fragile-x/fragile-x-syndrome/autism/.

- TSC Alliance: This organization offers information about autism and tuberous sclerosis complex at https://www.tscalliance.org/about-tsc/signs-and-symptoms-of-tsc/brain-and-neurological-function/tsc-and-autism-spectrum-disorders/.

Chapter Four

- Anxiety and Depression Association of America: Find information about autism and co-occurring depression and anxiety at https://adaa.org/understanding-anxiety/autism-anxiety-depression.
- National Association for the Dually Diagnosed: Their *Diagnostic Manual—Intellectual Disability-2* is available at https://thenadd.org/products/dm-id-2/.
- *Frontiers in Psychiatry*: The article "Sleep Disturbances in Children Affected by Autism Spectrum Disorder" is available at https://www.frontiersin.org/articles/10.3389/fpsyt.2022.736696/full, and the article "Sleep Problems in Children With Autism Spectrum Disorder in Hong Kong: A Cross-Sectional Study" is available at https://www.frontiersin.org/articles/10.3389/fpsyt.2023.1088209/full.
- UK National Autistic Society: Their mental health hub related to autism is at https://www.autism.org.uk/advice-and-guidance/topics/mental-health, and they offer insights about eating disorders at https://www.autism.org.uk/advice-and-guidance/topics/mental-health/eating-disorders.

Chapter Five

- The Program for the Education and Enrichment of Relational Skills at the University of California, Los Angeles: https://www.semel.ucla.edu/peers.
- *Teen Vogue* pulled together narratives of autistic teens and their dating experiences in their article, "What It's Like to Date When You're Autistic," available at https://www.teenvogue.com/story/dating-when-autistic.
- University College London's *Rough Guide to Social Media Use for Teens With Autism* is available at https://www.ucl.ac.uk/grand-challenges/sites/grand-challenges/files/rough_guide_to_social_media_use.pdf.
- The UK's National Autistic Society's advice for supporting your autistic child in making friends is available at https://www.autism.org.uk/advice-and-guidance/topics/family-life-and-relationships/making-friends/parents-and-carers and their information about dealing with bullying can be found at https://www.autism.org.uk/advice-and-guidance/topics/bullying/bullying/parents.

Chapter Six

- Amaze.org offers a host of age-appropriate, accessible, memorable videos for teens who need to learn accurate, candid information about health, including puberty, and about healthy sexuality: https://amaze.org/
- Another site that offers excellent information in accessible formats is Scarleteen: https://www.scarleteen.com/
- The Australian parenting website Raising Children offers tips on preparing autistic children for puberty: https://raisingchildren.net.au/autism/development/physical-development/preparing-for-puberty-asd
- The Center for Parent Information & Resources maintains an information center for sexuality education for young people with disabilities at https://www.parentcenterhub.org/sexed/.
- Vanderbilt Kennedy Center offers two publications about health and hygiene for this age, one for boys, at https://vkc.vumc.org/healthybodies/files/HealthyBodies-Boys-web.pdf, and another for girls, at https://vkc.vumc.org/healthybodies/files/HealthyBodies-Girls-web.pdf.
- Visual support resources are available at several sites, including:
  - https://card.ufl.edu/resources/visual-supports/
  - https://do2learn.com/
- The journal *Pediatrics* has open-access guidelines on menstrual management for adolescents with disabilities at https://publications.aap.org/pediatrics/article/138/1/e20160295/52591/Menstrual-Management-for-Adolescents-With
- For the complexity of managing personal hygiene, apps such as Goblin Tools (https://goblin.tools/) have proved useful for some autistic teens.

Chapter Seven

- Amaze.org offers a host of age-appropriate, accessible, memorable videos for teens who need to learn accurate, candid information about health, including puberty, and about healthy sexuality: https://amaze.org/
- Another site that offers excellent information in accessible formats is Scarleteen: https://www.scarleteen.com/
- The Australian parenting website Raising Children offers tips on preparing autistic children for puberty: https://raisingchildren.net.au/autism/development/physical-development/preparing-for-puberty-asd
- The Center for Parent Information & Resources maintains an information center for sexuality education for young people with disabilities at https://www.parentcenterhub.org/sexed/.

- Common Sense Media maintains information for parents about how to handle pornography at school and at home: https://www.commonsense.org/education/articles/how-to-handle-pornography-at-school-and-at-home
- The Crehan Lab at Tufts University maintains a website listing sexuality education resources for autistic people and their families at https://sites.tufts.edu/crehanlab/sex-ed-resource-list/.
- Family Planning Australia has material available online regarding masturbation information for people who have an intellectual disability at https://www.fpnsw.org.au/aboutmasturbation.
- The Organization for Autism Research offers several resources related to sexuality education for autistic people, including:
  - *Sex Ed for Self Advocates*: https://researchautism.org/self-advocates/sex-ed-for-self-advocates/
  - *Getting and Giving Consent for People With Autism*: https://researchautism.org/webinars/getting-and-giving-consent-for-people-with-autism/
  - A webinar for sexuality on the spectrum: https://researchautism.org/webinars/sexuality-on-the-spectrum/
  - A webinar on romantic relationships: https://sparkforautism.org/discover/tags/romantic-relationships/
  - Guidance for autistic people about consent: https://researchautism.org/wp-content/uploads/2023/04/What-is-Consent.pdf
- SIECUS: Sex Ed for Social Change offers a publication, *Comprehensive Sex Education for Youth With Disabilities*, available at https://siecus.org/wp-content/uploads/2021/03/SIECUS-2021-Youth-with-Disabilities-CTA-1.pdf.

Chapter Eight

- AbilityFirst has a College to Career program for autistic young people: https://www.abilityfirst.org/
- A listing of state vocational rehabilitation agencies: https://askearn.org/state-vocational-rehabilitation-agencies/
- Administration for Community Living: More information is available on the government website: https://acl.gov/about-acl/administration-disabilities
- The Autistic Self Advocacy Network's 2016 transition planning notebook: https://autisticadvocacy.org/wp-content/uploads/2016/11/Roadmap-to-Transition-A-Handbook-for-Autistic-Youth-Transitioning-to-Adulthood.pdf
- The College Living Experience site, with information to support neurodivergent college students: https://experiencecle.com/

- The Center on Secondary Education for Students With Autism Spectrum Disorder has a host of transition program materials available online: https://csesa.fpg.unc.edu/professionals/supporting-transition
- Information about Planning Alternative Tomorrows: https://participedia.net/method/5188
- National Adult Protective Services Association: https://www.napsa-now.org/help-in-your-area
- National Disability Rights Network's website, with information about protection and advocacy agencies: https://www.ndrn.org/about/ndrn-member-agencies/
- The National Resource Center for Supported Decision-Making offers resources and information about the meaning and application of this model: https://supporteddecisionmaking.org/
- Pathful offers the opportunity to do virtual job shadowing: https://pathful.com/explore
- The Organization for Autism Research's *A Guide for Transition to Adulthood* is available online at https://researchautism.org/resources/a-guide-for-transition-to-adulthood/.
- Search site for postsecondary programs for people with intellectual disabilities: https://thinkcollege.net/college-search
- Seattle University has a collection of different transition assessments here: https://www.seattleu.edu/ccts/resources/assessment/
- The University of Indiana has a lengthy article discussing various possible academic supports for autistic college students: https://www.iidc.indiana.edu/irca/articles/academic-supports-for-college-students-with-an-autism-spectrum-disorder.html
- University of Vermont website with information about Making Action Plans for Students: https://www.uvm.edu/sites/default/files/CDCI-Interdisciplinary-Team-I-Team/MAPSQuickFacts.pdf
- U.S. Department of Education's listing of state special education agencies: https://www2.ed.gov/about/contacts/state/index.html
- U.S. Department of Education: This agency maintains a links database where you can search for the proper special education agency for your state or region: https://www2.ed.gov/about/contacts/state/index.html

Bibliography

Aitken, D., & Fletcher-Watson, S. (2022, December 15). *Neurodiversity-affirmative education: Why and how.* The British Psychological Society. https://www.bps.org.uk/psychologist/neurodiversity-affirmative-education-why-and-how

Alhujaili, N., Platt, E., Khalid-Khan, S., & Groll, D. (2022). Comparison of social media use among adolescents with autism spectrum disorder and non-ASD adolescents. *Adolescent Health, Medicine and Therapeutics, 13*, 15–21. https://doi.org/10.2147/AHMT.S344591

Allely, C. S., Wilson, P., Minnis, H., Thompson, L., Yaksic, E., & Gillberg, C. (2017). Violence is rare in autism: When it does occur, is it sometimes extreme? *The Journal of Psychology, 151*(1), 49–68. https://doi.org/10.1080/00223980.2016.1175998

American Psychological Association. (2022). *DSM-5-TR and diagnoses for children.* https://www.psychiatry.org/getmedia/178f173b-f4a1-433b-aef3-7b2fb513436b/APA-DSM5TR-DiagnosesforChildren.pdf

Ames, J. L., Morgan, E. H., Onaiwu, M. G., Qian, Y., Massolo, M. L., & Croen, L. A. (2022). Racial/ethnic differences in psychiatric and medical diagnoses among autistic adults. *Autism in Adulthood: Challenges and Management, 4*(4), 290–305. https://doi.org/10.1089/aut.2021.0083

Andrews, L., Dees, R., & McIntyre, N. (2021, September). *Autism in females.* University of North Carolina, Frank Porter Graham Child Development Institute, CSESA Development Team.

Angell, A. M., Deavenport-Saman, A., Yin, L., Zou, B., Bai, C., Varma, D., & Solomon, O. (2021). Sex differences in co-occurring conditions among autistic children and youth in Florida: A retrospective cohort study (2012–2019). *Journal of Autism and Developmental Disorders, 51*(10), 3759–3765. https://doi.org/10.1007/s10803-020-04841-5

Antezana, L., Valdespino, A., Wieckowski, A. T., Coffman, M. C., Carlton, C. N., Garcia, K. M., Gracanin, D., White, S. W., & Richey, J. A. (2024). Social anxiety symptoms predict poorer facial emotion recognition in autistic male adolescents and young adults without intellectual disability. *Journal of Autism and Developmental Disorders*, 54(7), 2454–2470. https://doi.org/10.1007/s10803-023-05998-5

Autistic Self Advocacy Network. (2017). *Autism and safety toolkit: Safety tips for self-advocates*. https://autisticadvocacy.org/policy/toolkits/safety/

Autistic Self Advocacy Network. (2021a). *Functioning labels harm autistic people*. https://autisticadvocacy.org/2021/12/functioning-labels-harm-autistic-people/

Autistic Self Advocacy Network. (2021b). *Learn how colleges can help autistic students succeed with our new white paper!* https://autisticadvocacy.org/2021/03/learn-how-colleges-can-help-autistic-students-succeed-with-our-new-white-paper/

Baribeau, D. A., Vigod, S., Pullenayegum, E., Kerns, C. M., Mirenda, P., Smith, I. M., Vaillancourt, T., Volden, J., Waddell, C., Zwaigenbaum, L., Bennett, T., Duku, E., Elsabbagh, M., Georgiades, S., Ungar, W. J., Zaidman-Zait, A., & Szatmari, P. (2020). Repetitive behavior severity as an early indicator of risk for elevated anxiety symptoms in autism spectrum disorder. *Journal of the American Academy of Child and Adolescent Psychiatry*, 59(7), 890–899.e3. https://doi.org/10.1016/j.jaac.2019.08.478

Beckman, L., Hellström, L., & von Kobyletzki, L. (2020). Cyber bullying among children with neurodevelopmental disorders: A systematic review. *Scandinavian Journal of Psychology*, 61(1), 54–67. https://doi.org/10.1111/sjop.12525

Besag, F. M. (2018). Epilepsy in patients with autism: Links, risks and treatment challenges. *Neuropsychiatric Disease and Treatment*, 14, 1–10. https://doi.org/10.2147/NDT.S120509

Bishop, L., McLean, K. J., & Rubenstein, E. (2021). Epilepsy in adulthood: Prevalence, incidence, and associated antiepileptic drug use in autistic adults in a state Medicaid system. *Autism: The International Journal of Research and Practice*, 25(3), 831–839. https://doi.org/10.1177/1362361320942982

Blajwajs, L., Williams, J., Timmons, W., & Sproule, J. (2023). Hypermobility prevalence, measurements, and outcomes in childhood, adolescence, and emerging adulthood: A systematic review. *Rheumatology International*, 43(8), 1423–1444. https://doi.org/10.1007/s00296-023-05338-x

Bolourian, Y., Stavropoulos, K. K. M., Blacher, J. (2019). Autism in the classroom: Educational issues across the lifespan. In *Autism Spectrum Disorders—Advances at the End of the Second Decade of the 21st Century*, Ed. Fitzgerald, M. https://www.intechopen.com/chapters/65947

Bozhilova, N., Welham, A., Adams, D., Bissell, S., Bruining, H., Crawford, H., Eden, K., Nelson, L., Oliver, C., Powis, L., Richards, C., Waite, J., Watson, P., Rhys, H., Wilde, L., Woodcock, K., & Moss, J. (2023). Profiles of autism characteristics in thirteen genetic syndromes: A machine learning approach. *Molecular Autism, 14*(1), 3. https://doi.org/10.1186/s13229-022-00530-5

Bradley, L., Shaw, R., Baron-Cohen, S., & Cassidy, S. (2021). Autistic adults' experiences of camouflaging and its perceived impact on mental health. *Autism in Adulthood: Challenges and Management, 3*(4), 320–329. https://doi.org/10.1089/aut.2020.0071

Brunissen, L., Rapoport, E., Chawarska, K., & Adesman, A. (2021). Sex differences in gender-diverse expressions and identities among youth with autism spectrum disorder. *Autism Research: Official Journal of the International Society for Autism Research, 14*(1), 143–155. https://doi.org/10.1002/aur.2441

Bush, H. H., Williams, L. W., & Mendes, E. (2021). Brief report: Asexuality and young women on the autism spectrum. *Journal of Autism and Developmental Disorders, 51*(2), 725–733. https://doi.org/10.1007/s10803-020-04565-6

Campbell, K., Holderness, N., & Riggs, M. (2015). Friendship chemistry: An examination of underlying factors. *The Social Science Journal, 52*(2), 239–247. https://doi.org/10.1016/j.soscij.2015.01.005

Capozzi, S., Barmache, D., Cladis, E., Peña, E. V., & Kocur, J. (2019). The significance of involving nonspeaking autistic peer mentors in educational programs. *Autism in Adulthood: Challenges and Management, 1*(3), 170–172. https://doi.org/10.1089/aut.2019.0006

Carter Leno, V., Micali, N., Bryant-Waugh, R., & Herle, M. (2022). Associations between childhood autistic traits and adolescent eating disorder behaviours are partially mediated by fussy eating. *European Eating Disorders Review: The Journal of the Eating Disorders Association, 30*(5), 604–615. https://doi.org/10.1002/erv.2902

Cazalis, F., Reyes, E., Leduc, S., & Gourion, D. (2022). Evidence that nine autistic women out of ten have been victims of sexual violence. *Frontiers in Behavioral Neuroscience, 16*, 852203. https://doi.org/10.3389/fnbeh.2022.852203

Centers for Disease Control and Prevention. *Estimated number of adults living with autism spectrum disorder in the United States, 2017*. https://archive.cdc.gov/#/details?url=https://www.cdc.gov/autism/publications/adults-living-with-autism-spectrum-disorder.html

Centers for Disease Control and Prevention. (2024). *Heavy menstrual bleeding*. https://www.cdc.gov/female-blood-disorders/about/heavy-menstrual-bleeding.html

Children's Hospital of Philadelphia. (2020). *Intellectual disability and ASD*. CHOP Research Institute. https://research.chop.edu/car-autism-roadmap/intellectual-disability-and-asd

Cho, S., Cola, M., Knox, A., Pelella, M. R., Russell, A., Hauptmann, A., Covello, M., Cieri, C., Liberman, M., Schultz, R. T., & Parish-Morris, J. (2023). Sex differences in the temporal dynamics of autistic children's natural conversations. *Molecular Autism, 14*(1), 13. https://doi.org/10.1186/s13229-023-00545-6

Clairmont, C., Wang, J., Tariq, S., Sherman, H. T., Zhao, M., & Kong, X. J. (2022). The value of brain imaging and electrophysiological testing for early screening of autism spectrum disorder: A systematic review. *Frontiers in Neuroscience, 15*, 812946. https://doi.org/10.3389/fnins.2021.812946

Clinard, A. (2016, February). *Internet safety for teens with ASD*. University of North Carolina, Frank Porter Graham Child Development Institute, CSESA Development Team.

Clothier, J., & Absoud, M. (2021). Autism spectrum disorder and kidney disease. *Pediatric Nephrology (Berlin, Germany), 36*(10), 2987–2995. https://doi.org/10.1007/s00467-020-04875-y

Cochran, L., Moss, J., Nelson, L., & Oliver, C. (2015). Contrasting age related changes in autism spectrum disorder phenomenology in Cornelia de Lange, fragile X, and Cri du Chat syndromes: Results from a 2.5 year follow-up. *American Journal of Medical Genetics. Part C, Seminars in Medical Genetics, 169*(2), 188–197. https://doi.org/10.1002/ajmg.c.31438

Coffey, B., & Luber, M. (2019). Definition and DSM-5: Classification: Tic disorders. https://www.news-medical.net/health/Definition-and-DSM-5-Classification-Tic-Disorders.aspx

Cola, M., Zampella, C. J., Yankowitz, L. D., Plate, S., Petrulla, V., Tena, K., Russell, A., Pandey, J., Schultz, R. T., & Parish-Morris, J. (2022). Conversational adaptation in children and teens with autism: Differences in talkativeness across contexts. *Autism Research: Official Journal of the International Society for Autism Research, 15*(6), 1090–1108. https://doi.org/10.1002/aur.2693

Collins, J., Horton, K., Gale-St Ives, E., Murphy, G., & Barnoux, M. (2023). A systematic review of autistic people and the criminal justice system: An update of King and Murphy (2014). *Journal of Autism and Developmental Disorders, 53*(8), 3151–3179. https://doi.org/10.1007/s10803-022-05590-3

Corbett, B. A., Muscatello, R. A., Kim, A., Vandekar, S., Duffus, S., Sparks, S., & Tanguturi, Y. (2022). Examination of pubertal timing and tempo in females and males with autism spectrum disorder compared to typically developing youth. *Autism Research: Official Journal of the International Society for Autism Research, 15*(10), 1894–1908. https://doi.org/10.1002/aur.2786

Corbett, B. A., Muscatello, R. A., Tanguturi, Y., McGinn, E., & Ioannou, S. (2019). Pubertal development measurement in children with and without autism spectrum disorder: A comparison between physical exam, parent- and self-report. *Journal of Autism and Developmental Disorders, 49*(12), 4807–4819. https://doi.org/10.1007/s10803-019-04192-w

Corbett, B. A., Vandekar, S., Muscatello, R. A., & Tanguturi, Y. (2020). Pubertal timing during early adolescence: Advanced pubertal onset in females with autism spectrum disorder. *Autism Research: Official Journal of the International Society for Autism Research, 13*(12), 2202–2215. https://doi.org/10.1002/aur.2406

Coulter, D., Lynch, C., & Joosten, A. V. (2023). Exploring the perspectives of young adults with developmental disabilities about sexuality and sexual health education. *Australian Occupational Therapy Journal, 70*(3), 380–391. https://doi.org/10.1111/1440-1630.12862

Crehan, E. T., Rocha, J., Sclar, J., Ward, O., & Donaghue, A. (2023). Topics and timing of sexuality and relationship education for autistic and non-autistic adults in the United States. *Disability and Health Journal, 16*(3), 101466. https://doi.org/10.1016/j.dhjo.2023.101466

Crehan, E. T., Yang, X., Dufresne, S., Barstein, J., Stephens, L., Dekker, L., & Greaves-Lord, K. (2024). Adapting the Tackling Teenage Training Sex Education Program for Autistic Adults in the US: A pilot study. *Journal of Autism and Developmental Disorders, 54*(6), 2108–2123. https://doi.org/10.1007/s10803-023-05962-3

Csecs, J. L. L., Iodice, V., Rae, C. L., Brooke, A., Simmons, R., Quadt, L., Savage, G. K., Dowell, N. G., Prowse, F., Themelis, K., Mathias, C. J., Critchley, H. D., & Eccles, J. A. (2022). Joint hypermobility links neurodivergence to dysautonomia and pain. *Frontiers in Psychiatry, 12*, 786916. https://doi.org/10.3389/fpsyt.2021.786916

Cummins, C., Pellicano, E., & Crane, L. (2020). Supporting minimally verbal autistic girls with intellectual disabilities through puberty: Perspectives of parents and educators. *Journal of Autism and Developmental Disorders, 50*(7), 2439–2448. https://doi.org/10.1007/s10803-018-3782-8

Curry, A. E., Yerys, B. E., Huang, P., & Metzger, K. B. (2018). Longitudinal study of driver licensing rates among adolescents and young adults with autism spectrum disorder. *Autism : The International Journal of Research and Practice, 22*(4), 479–488. https://doi.org/10.1177/1362361317699586

DaWalt, L. S., Fielding-Gebhardt, H., Fleming, K. K., Warren, S. F., & Brady, N. (2022). Change in behavior problems from childhood through adolescence for children with fragile X syndrome. *Journal of Autism and Developmental Disorders, 52*(9), 4056–4066. https://doi.org/10.1007/s10803-021-05270-8

Dewinter, J., De Graaf, H., & Begeer, S. (2017). Sexual orientation, gender identity, and romantic relationships in adolescents and adults with autism spectrum disorder. *Journal of Autism and Developmental Disorders, 47*(9), 2927–2934. https://doi.org/10.1007/s10803-017-3199-9

Diddy, J. (2022). *An inclusive guide to puberty and periods*. Cedars Sinai. https://www.cedars-sinai.org/blog/inclusive-guide-puberty-and-periods.html

Eagle, C. (2021). *How to empower youth for employment & adult life*. https://researchautism.org/audience/education/how-to-empower-youth-for-employment-and-adult-life/

Earp, B. D., Monrad, J. T., LaFrance, M., Bargh, J. A., Cohen, L. L., & Richeson, J. A. (2019). Featured article: Gender bias in pediatric pain assessment. *Journal of Pediatric Psychology, 44*(4), 403–414.

Elias, R., & Lord, C. (2022). Diagnostic stability in individuals with autism spectrum disorder: Insights from a longitudinal follow-up study. *Journal of Child Psychology and Psychiatry, and Allied Disciplines, 63*(9), 973–983.

Epilepsy Foundation. (2017). *Epilepsy and autism: Is there a relationship?* https://www.epilepsy.com/stories/epilepsy-and-autism-there-relationship

Fink, D. A., Nelson, L. M., Pyeritz, R., Johnson, J., Sherman, S. L., Cohen, Y., & Elizur, S. E. (2018). Fragile X associated primary ovarian insufficiency (FXPOI): Case report and literature review. *Frontiers in Genetics, 9*, 529. https://doi.org/10.3389/fgene.2018.00529

Flax, J., Gwin, C., Wilson, S., Fradkin, Y., Buyske, S., & Brzustowicz, L. (2019). Social (pragmatic) communication disorder: Another name for the broad autism phenotype?. *Autism: The International Journal of Research and Practice, 23*(8), 1982–1992.

Fountain, C., Winter, A. S., & Bearman, P. S. (2012). Six developmental trajectories characterize children with autism. *Pediatrics, 129*(5), e1112–e1120. https://doi.org/10.1542/peds.2011-1601

Friskney, R., Tisdall, E. K. M., & Aitken, D. (2019). *Communication matters: Three scoping studies about the experiences of children with learning difficulties, and their families, in Scotland.* https://edwebcontent.ed.ac.uk/sites/default/files/atoms/files/mh-cys-1-communication-matters.pdf

Gavidia, M. (2020). *Addressing sleep issues in children, teens with autism.* American Journal of Managed Care. https://www.ajmc.com/view/addressing-sleep-issues-in-children-teens-with-autism

George, R., & Stokes, M. A. (2018). Gender identity and sexual orientation in autism spectrum disorder. *Autism: The International Journal of Research and Practice, 22*(8), 970–982. https://doi.org/10.1177/1362361317714587

Glans, M. R., Thelin, N., Humble, M. B., Elwin, M., & Bejerot, S. (2022). The relationship between generalised joint hypermobility and autism spectrum disorder in adults: A large, cross-sectional, case control comparison. *Frontiers in Psychiatry, 12*, 803334. https://doi.org/10.3389/fpsyt.2021.803334

Gotham, K., Brunwasser, S. M., & Lord, C. (2015). Depressive and anxiety symptom trajectories from school age through young adulthood in samples with autism spectrum disorder and developmental delay. *Journal of the American Academy of Child and Adolescent Psychiatry, 54*(5), 369–76.e3. https://doi.org/10.1016/j.jaac.2015.02.005

Graham Holmes, L., Rast, J. E., Roux, A. M., & Rothman, E. F. (2022). Reproductive health and substance use education for autistic youth. *Pediatrics, 149*(Suppl. 4), e2020049437T. https://doi.org/10.1542/peds.2020-049437T

Habayeb, S., Kenworthy, L., de La Torre, A., & Ratto, A. (2022). Still left behind: Fewer Black school-aged youth receive ASD diagnoses compared to White youth. *Journal of Autism and Developmental Disorders, 52*(5), 2274–2283. https://doi.org/10.1007/s10803-021-05118-1

Hall, J. P., Batza, K., Streed, C. G., Jr., Boyd, B. A., & Kurth, N. K. (2020). Health disparities among sexual and gender minorities with autism spectrum disorder. *Journal of Autism and Developmental Disorders, 50*(8), 3071–3077. https://doi.org/10.1007/s10803-020-04399-2

Helverschou, B., Bakken, B. L., Martinsen, H. (2009). The Psychopathology in Autism Checklist (PAC): A pilot study. *Research in Autism Spectrum Disorders.* https://doi.org/10.1016/j.rasd.2008.05.004

Hess, P. (2022). *DSM-5 revision tweaks autism entry for clarity.* The Transmitter. https://www.thetransmitter.org/spectrum/dsm-5-revision-tweaks-autism-entry-for-clarity/

Hill, A. P., Zuckerman, K. E., & Fombonne, E. (2015). Obesity and autism. *Pediatrics, 136*(6), 1051–1061. https://doi.org/10.1542/peds.2015-1437

Holden, R., Mueller, J., McGowan, J., Sanyal, J., Kikoler, M., Simonoff, E., Velupillai, S., & Downs, J. (2020). Investigating bullying as a predictor of suicidality in a clinical sample of adolescents with autism spectrum disorder. *Autism Research: Official Journal of the International Society for Autism Research, 13*(6), 988–997. https://doi.org/10.1002/aur.2292

Holingue, C., Kalb, L. G., Musci, R., Lukens, C., Lee, L. C., Kaczaniuk, J., Landrum, M., Buie, T., & Fallin, M. D. (2022). Characteristics of the autism spectrum disorder gastrointestinal and related behaviors inventory in children. *Autism Research: Official Journal of the International Society for Autism Research, 15*(6), 1142–1155. https://doi.org/10.1002/aur.2707

Hollocks, M. J., Lerh, J. W., Magiati, I., Meiser-Stedman, R., & Brugha, T. S. (2019). Anxiety and depression in adults with autism spectrum disorder: A systematic review and meta-analysis. *Psychological Medicine, 49*(4), 559–572. https://doi.org/10.1017/S0033291718002283

Holmes, L. G., Strassberg, D. S., & Himle, M. B. (2019). Family sexuality communication for adolescent girls on the autism spectrum. *Journal of Autism and Developmental Disorders, 49*(6), 2403–2416. https://doi.org/10.1007/s10803-019-03904-6

Hong, J., DaWalt, L. S., Taylor, J. L., Haider, A., & Mailick, M. (2023). Autism through midlife: Trajectories of symptoms, behavioral functioning, and health. *Journal of Neurodevelopmental Disorders, 15*(1), 36.

Houtrow, A., Elias, E. R., Davis, B. E., & Council on Children With Disabilities. (2021). Promoting healthy sexuality for children and adolescents with disabilities. *Pediatrics, 148*(1), e2021052043. https://doi.org/10.1542/peds.2021-052043

Hunter, J., Rivero-Arias, O., Angelov, A., Kim, E., Fotheringham, I., & Leal, J. (2014). Epidemiology of fragile X syndrome: A systematic review and meta-analysis. *American Journal of Medical Genetics. Part A, 164A*(7), 1648–1658.

Iversen, S., & Kildahl, A. N. (2022). Case report: Mechanisms in misdiagnosis of autism as borderline personality disorder. *Frontiers in Psychology, 13*, 735205. https://doi.org/10.3389/fpsyg.2022.735205

Jansson, A. K., Söderling, J., Reutfors, J., Thor, A., Sköld, C., Cohn-Cedermark, G., Ståhl, O., Smedby, K. E., Pettersson, A., & Glimelius, I. (2023). Risk and mortality of testicular cancer in patients with neurodevelopmental or other psychiatric disorders. *British Journal of Cancer*, *128*(12), 2261–2269. https://doi.org/10.1038/s41416-023-02260-8

Joyal, C. C., Carpentier, J., McKinnon, S., Normand, C. L., & Poulin, M. H. (2021). Sexual knowledge, desires, and experience of adolescents and young adults with an autism spectrum disorder: An exploratory study. *Frontiers in Psychiatry*, *12*, 685256. https://doi.org/10.3389/fpsyt.2021.685256

Käld, E., Beckman, L., Eapen, V., & Lin, P. I. (2022). Exploring potential modifiers of the association between neurodevelopmental disorders and risk of bullying exposure. *JAMA Pediatrics*, *176*(9), 940–941. https://doi.org/10.1001/jamapediatrics.2022.1755

Kallitsounaki, A., & Williams, D. M. (2023). Autism spectrum disorder and gender dysphoria/incongruence. A systematic literature review and meta-analysis. *Journal of Autism and Developmental Disorders*, *53*(8), 3103–3117. https://doi.org/10.1007/s10803-022-05517-y

Kanfiszer, L., Davies, F., & Collins, S. (2017). "I was just so different": The experiences of women diagnosed with an autism spectrum disorder in adulthood in relation to gender and social relationships. *Autism: The International Journal of Research and Practice*, *21*(6), 661–669.

Kildahl, A. N., Bakken, T. L., Matre, E. A. W., Hellerud, J. M. A., Engebretsen, M. H., & Helverschou, S. B. (2020). Case study: Identification of anxiety and subsequent intervention in an adolescent male with autism, severe intellectual disability and self-injurious behaviour. *International Journal of Developmental Disabilities*, *67*(5), 327–338. https://doi.org/10.1080/20473869.2020.1850160

Kinnaird, E., Sedgewick, F., Stewart, C., & Tchanturia, K. (2019). Exploring self-reported eating disorder symptoms in autistic men. *Autism in Adulthood: Challenges and Management*, *1*(4), 306–310. https://doi.org/10.1089/aut.2019.0017

Kim, Y. S., Leventhal, B. L., Koh, Y. J., Fombonne, E., Laska, E., Lim, E. C., Cheon, K. A., Kim, S. J., Kim, Y. K., Lee, H., Song, D. H., & Grinker, R. R. (2011). Prevalence of autism spectrum disorders in a total population sample. *The American Journal of Psychiatry*, *168*(9), 904–912.

Klusek, J., Will, E., Moser, C., Hills, K., Thurman, A. J., Abbeduto, L., & Roberts, J. E. (2023). Predictors, parental views, and concordance across diagnostic sources of autism in male youth with fragile X syndrome: Clinical best estimate and community diagnoses. *Research on Child and Adolescent Psychopathology*, *51*(7), 989–1004. https://doi.org/10.1007/s10802-023-01044-1

Kulage, K. M., Goldberg, J., Usseglio, J., Romero, D., Bain, J. M., & Smaldone, A. M. (2020). How has DSM-5 affected autism diagnosis? A 5-year follow-up systematic literature review and meta-analysis. *Journal of Autism and Developmental Disorders, 50*(6), 2102–2127.

Lai, M. C., Kassee, C., Besney, R., Bonato, S., Hull, L., Mandy, W., Szatmari, P., & Ameis, S. H. (2019). Prevalence of co-occurring mental health diagnoses in the autism population: A systematic review and meta-analysis. *The Lancet: Psychiatry, 6*(10), 819–829. https://doi.org/10.1016/S2215-0366(19)30289-

Laugeson, E. A., Frankel, F., Mogil, C., & Dillon, A. R. (2009). Parent-assisted social skills training to improve friendships in teens with autism spectrum disorders. *Journal of Autism and Developmental Disorders, 39*(4), 596–606. https://doi.org/10.1007/s10803-008-0664-5

Leader, G., Hogan, A., Chen, J. L., Maher, L., Naughton, K., O'Rourke, N., Casburn, M., & Mannion, A. (2022). Age of autism spectrum disorder diagnosis and comorbidity in children and adolescents with autism spectrum disorder. *Developmental Neurorehabilitation, 25*(1), 29–37. https://doi.org/10.1080/17518423.2021.1917717

Lecavalier, L., McCracken, C. E., Aman, M. G., McDougle, C. J., McCracken, J. T., Tierney, E., Smith, T., Johnson, C., King, B., Handen, B., Swiezy, N. B., Eugene Arnold, L., Bearss, K., Vitiello, B., & Scahill, L. (2019). An exploration of concomitant psychiatric disorders in children with autism spectrum disorder. *Comprehensive Psychiatry, 88*, 57–64. https://doi.org/10.1016/j.comppsych.2018.10.012

Lerner, M. D., Mikami, A. Y., & Levine, K. (2011). Socio-dramatic affective-relational intervention for adolescents with Asperger syndrome & high functioning autism: Pilot study. *Autism: The International Journal of Research and Practice, 15*(1), 21–42. https://doi.org/10.1177/1362361309353613

Li, C., & He, W. Q. (2022). Trends in autism spectrum disorder among children and adolescents in the US from 2016 to 2020. *JAMA Pediatrics, 176*(12), 1270–1271. https://doi.org/10.1001/jamapediatrics.2022.4109

Li, Q., Li, Y., Liu, B., Chen, Q., Xing, X., Xu, G., & Yang, W. (2022). Prevalence of autism spectrum disorder among children and adolescents in the United States from 2019 to 2020. *JAMA Pediatrics, 176*(9), 943–945.

Libster, N., Knox, A., Engin, S., Geschwind, D., Parish-Morris, J., & Kasari, C. (2023). Sex differences in friendships and loneliness in autistic and non-autistic children across development. *Molecular Autism, 14*(1), 9. https://doi.org/10.1186/s13229-023-00542-9

Lin, P.D. & Eapen, V. (2022). *Kids on the autism spectrum experience more bullying. Schools can do something about it.* The Conversation. https://theconversation.com/kids-on-the-autism-spectrum-experience-more-bullying-schools-can-do-something-about-it-184385

Lukmanji, S., Manji, S. A., Kadhim, S., Sauro, K. M., Wirrell, E. C., Kwon, C. S., & Jetté, N. (2019). The co-occurrence of epilepsy and autism: A systematic review. *Epilepsy & Behavior: E&B, 98*(Pt. A), 238–248. https://doi.org/10.1016/j.yebeh.2019.07.037

Lundy, K. M., Wenzbauer, M. A., Illapperuma, C. R., Fischer, A. J., Feng, M. J., Jensen, R. L., Maldonado, A. F., Mathis, S. N., Meservy, J. O., & Heller, H. N. (2022). Evaluating the acceptability and social validity of a caregiver-led technology-based menstrual hygiene management intervention for youth on the autism spectrum. *Advances in Neurodevelopmental Disorders*, *6*(3), 315–330. https://doi.org/10.1007/s41252-022-00261-x

Maenner, M. J., Shaw, K. A., Bakian, A. V., Bilder, D. A., Durkin, M. S., Esler, A., Furnier, S. M., Hallas, L., Hall-Lande, J., Hudson, A., Hughes, M. M., Patrick, M., Pierce, K., Poynter, J. N., Salinas, A., Shenouda, J., Vehorn, A., Warren, Z., Constantino, J. N., . . . Cogswell, M. E. (2021). Prevalence and characteristics of autism spectrum disorder among children aged 8 years—Autism and Developmental Disabilities Monitoring Network, 11 Sites, United States, 2018. *Morbidity and Mortality Weekly Report*, *70*(11), 1–16. https://doi.org/10.15585/mmwr.ss7011a1

Malone, P. (Ed.). (2016). *Roadmap to transition: A handbook for autistic youth transitioning to adulthood*. Autistic Self Advocacy Network. https://autisticadvocacy.org/book/roadmap/

Mandy, W., Midouhas, E., Hosozawa, M., Cable, N., Sacker, A., & Flouri, E. (2022). Mental health and social difficulties of late-diagnosed autistic children, across childhood and adolescence. *Journal of Child Psychology and Psychiatry, and Allied Disciplines*, *63*(11), 1405–1414. https://doi.org/10.1111/jcpp.13587

Martin, A. F., Jassi, A., Cullen, A. E., Broadbent, M., Downs, J., & Krebs, G. (2020). Co-occurring obsessive-compulsive disorder and autism spectrum disorder in young people: Prevalence, clinical characteristics and outcomes. *European Child & Adolescent Psychiatry*, *29*(11), 1603–1611. https://doi.org/10.1007/s00787-020-01478-8

McCauley, J. B., Elias, R., & Lord, C. (2020). Trajectories of co-occurring psychopathology symptoms in autism from late childhood to adulthood. *Development and Psychopathology*, *32*(4), 1287–1302. https://doi.org/10.1017/S0954579420000826

McGuire, K., & Veenstra-VanderWeele, J. (2020). Editorial: Important first look at population-based trajectories of youths with autism. *Journal of the American Academy of Child and Adolescent Psychiatry*, *59*(12), 1321–1323. https://doi.org/10.1016/j.jaac.2020.06.011

McIntyre, N., & Harrah, M. (2020, May). *Using public transportation*. University of North Carolina, Frank Porter Graham Child Development Institute, CSESA Development Team. https://fpg.unc.edu/publications/autism-glance-using-public-transportation

McMaughan, D. J. D., Jones, J. L., Mulcahy, A., Tucker, E. C., Beverly, J. G., & Perez-Patron, M. (2022). Hospitalizations among children and youth with autism in the United States: Frequency, characteristics, and costs. *Intellectual and Developmental Disabilities*, *60*(6), 484–503. https://doi.org/10.1352/1934-9556-60.6.484

Mhatre, N. (2021). *Access, autonomy, and dignity: Comprehensive sexuality education for people with disabilities.* Autistic Self Advocacy Network. https://nationalpartnership.org/wp-content/uploads/2023/02/repro-disability-sexed.pdf

Micale, L., Fusco, C., & Castori, M. (2021). Ehlers–Danlos syndromes, joint hypermobility and hypermobility spectrum disorders. *Advances in Experimental Medicine and Biology, 1348*, 207–233. https://doi.org/10.1007/978-3-030-80614-9_9

MIT Tech Review. Emerging Technology. (2015). Your brain limits you to just five BFFs. *MIT Technology Review.* https://www.technologyreview.com/2016/04/29/160438/your-brain-limits-you-to-just-five-bffs/

Mogensen, L., & Mason, J. (2015). The meaning of a label for teenagers negotiating identity: Experiences with autism spectrum disorder. *Sociology of Health & Illness, 37*(2), 255–269. https://doi.org/10.1111/1467-9566.12208

Moua, P. (2016, January). *Puberty in adolescents with ASD.* University of North Carolina, Frank Porter Graham Child Development Institute, CSESA Development Team. https://fpg.unc.edu/publications/autism-glance-puberty-adolescents-asd

Mutluer, T., Aslan Genç, H., Özcan Morey, A., Yapici Eser, H., Ertinmaz, B., Can, M., & Munir, K. (2022). Population-based psychiatric comorbidity in children and adolescents with autism spectrum disorder: A meta-analysis. *Frontiers in Psychiatry, 13*, 856208. https://doi.org/10.3389/fpsyt.2022.856208

National Association for the Dually Diagnosed. (2018). *Diagnostic Manual—Intellectual Disability: A Clinical Guide for Diagnosis (DM-ID-2).* Fletcher, R. (Ed).

National Autistic Society. *Criteria and tools used in an autism assessment.* https://www.autism.org.uk/advice-and-guidance/topics/diagnosis/assessment-and-diagnosis/criteria-and-tools-used-in-an-autism-assessment.

National Fragile X Foundation. (2018). *FXPOI treatment recommendations.* https://fragilex.org/professional-resources/treatment-recommendations/fragile-x-associated-primary-ovarian-insufficiency/

National Institute of Child Health and Human Development. (2021). *Fragile X–associated primary ovarian insufficiency (FXPOI).* NICHD, Eunice Kennedy Shriver National Institute of Child Health and Human Development. https://www.nichd.nih.gov/health/topics/fxpoi

NPR/Kaiser/Kennedy School Poll. *Sex education in America.* https://www.kff.org/wp-content/uploads/2013/01/sex-education-in-america-summary.pdf.

Organization for Autism Research. (2018). *Sexuality on the spectrum.* https://researchautism.org/webinars/sexuality-on-the-spectrum/

Organization for Autism Research. (2021). *Life journey through autism: A guide for transition to adulthood.* https://researchautism.org/product/a-guide-for-transition-to-adulthood/

Organization for Autism Research. (2023). Getting and giving consent: For people with autism. https://researchautism.org/webinars/getting-and-giving-consent-for-people-with-autism/

Orth, T. (2023). *Despite data suggesting otherwise, many Americans think teen drinking and dating have increased*. YouGov. https://today.yougov.com/society/articles/44957-many-americans-think-teen-drinking-dating-increase

Pecora, L. A., Hooley, M., Sperry, L., Mesibov, G. B., & Stokes, M. A. (2020). Sexuality and gender issues in individuals with autism spectrum disorder. *Child and Adolescent Psychiatric Clinics of North America, 29*(3), 543–556. https://doi.org/10.1016/j.chc.2020.02.007

Pender, R., Fearon, P., St Pourcain, B., Heron, J., & Mandy, W. (2023). Developmental trajectories of autistic social traits in the general population. *Psychological Medicine, 53*(3), 814–822. https://doi.org/10.1017/S0033291721002166

Płatos, M., Wojaczek, K., & Laugeson, E. A. (2024). Fostering friendship and dating skills among adults on the autism spectrum: A randomized controlled trial of the Polish version of the PEERS® for Young Adults curriculum. *Journal of Autism and Developmental Disorders, 54*(6), 2224–2239. https://doi.org/10.1007/s10803-023-05921-y

Prigge, M. B. D., Bigler, E. D., Lange, N., Morgan, J., Froehlich, A., Freeman, A., Kellett, K., Kane, K. L., King, C. K., Taylor, J., Dean, D. C., 3rd, King, J. B., Anderson, J. S., Zielinski, B. A., Alexander, A. L., & Lainhart, J. E. (2022). Longitudinal stability of intellectual functioning in autism spectrum disorder: From age 3 through mid-adulthood. *Journal of Autism and Developmental Disorders, 52*(10), 4490–4504. https://doi.org/10.1007/s10803-021-05227-x

Rai, D., Heuvelman, H., Dalman, C., Culpin, I., Lundberg, M., Carpenter, P., & Magnusson, C. (2018). Association between autism spectrum disorders with or without intellectual disability and depression in young adulthood. *JAMA Network Open, 1*(4), e181465. https://doi.org/10.1001/jamanetworkopen.2018.1465

Reichow, B. & Volkmar, F. (2018). *Narrowing of "autism" in DSM-5 runs counter to idea of broad spectrum*. https://www.thetransmitter.org/spectrum/narrowing-autism-dsm-5-runs-counter-idea-broad-spectrum/

Reid, W. (2021). *Social media can provide connections for children and adults on the autism spectrum*. UVA Today. https://news.virginia.edu/content/social-media-can-provide-connections-children-and-adults-autism-spectrum

Rentschler, L. F., Hume, K. A., & Steinbrenner, J. R. (2022). Building inclusive high school communities for autistic students. *TEACHING Exceptional Children, 56*(2), 98–106. https://doi.org/10.1177/00400599221098194

Rodda, A., & Estes, A. (2018). Beyond social skills: Supporting peer relationships and friendships for school-aged children with autism spectrum disorder. *Seminars in Speech and Language, 39*(2), 178–194. https://doi.org/10.1055/s-0038-1628369

Rosa, S. D. (2020). *How to create social groups for autistic teens and adults*. Thinking Person's Guide to Autism. https://thinkingautismguide.com/2020/03/how-to-create-autistic-social-groups.html

Rosen, A. R. (2020). *Epilepsy and autism*. Practical Neurology. https://practicalneurology.com/articles/2020-oct/epilepsy-and-autism

Rosen, T. E., Mazefsky, C. A., Vasa, R. A., & Lerner, M. D. (2018). Co-occurring psychiatric conditions in autism spectrum disorder. *International Review of Psychiatry (Abingdon, England)*, *30*(1), 40–61. https://doi.org/10.1080/09540261.2018.1450229

Russell, I., Pearson, B., & Masic, U. (2021). A longitudinal study of features associated with autism spectrum in clinic referred, gender diverse adolescents accessing puberty suppression treatment. *Journal of Autism and Developmental Disorders*, *51*(6), 2068–2076. https://doi.org/10.1007/s10803-020-04698-8

Salem, J., & Kennedy, C. (2021). Obstacles to diagnostic investigation of a child with comorbid psychiatric conditions. *Scandinavian Journal of Child And Adolescent Psychiatry and Psychology*, *9*, 105–112.

Scheeren, A. M., Koot, H. M., & Begeer, S. (2020). Stability and change in social interaction style of children with autism spectrum disorder: A 4-year follow-up study. *Autism Research: Official Journal of the International Society for Autism Research*, *13*(1), 74–81. https://doi.org/10.1002/aur.2201

Simonoff, E., Kent, R., Stringer, D., Lord, C., Briskman, J., Lukito, S., Pickles, A., Charman, T., & Baird, G. (2020). Trajectories in symptoms of autism and cognitive ability in autism from childhood to adult life: Findings from a longitudinal epidemiological cohort. *Journal of the American Academy of Child and Adolescent Psychiatry*, *59*(12), 1342–1352. https://doi.org/10.1016/j.jaac.2019.11.020

Singer, E. (2023). *Sex education and autism*. SPARK for Autism. https://sparkforautism.org/discover_article/sex-education-and-autism/

Solberg, B. S., Zayats, T., Posserud, M. B., Halmøy, A., Engeland, A., Haavik, J., & Klungsøyr, K. (2019). Patterns of psychiatric comorbidity and genetic correlations provide new insights into differences between attention-deficit/hyperactivity disorder and autism spectrum disorder. *Biological Psychiatry*, *86*(8), 587–598. https://doi.org/10.1016/j.biopsych.2019.04.021

Solmi, F., Bentivegna, F., Bould, H., Mandy, W., Kothari, R., Rai, D., Skuse, D., & Lewis, G. (2021). Trajectories of autistic social traits in childhood and adolescence and disordered eating behaviours at age 14 years: A UK general population cohort study. *Journal of Child Psychology and Psychiatry, and Allied Disciplines*, *62*(1), 75–85. https://doi.org/10.1111/jcpp.13255

SPARK. (2022). *Preparing for puberty in children with autism*. https://sparkforautism.org/discover_article/webinar-puberty-autism/

Spectrum. (2021). *Puberty and autism: An unexplored transition*. The Transmitter. https://www.thetransmitter.org/spectrum/puberty-and-autism-an-unexplored-transition/

UK National Autistic Society. *What is self harm?* UK NAS. https://www.autism.org.uk/advice-and-guidance/topics/mental-health/self-harm#What%20is%20self-harm?

University College London. *Rough guide to social media use for teens with autism*. UCL. https://www.ucl.ac.uk/grand-challenges/sites/grand-challenges/files/rough_guide_to_social_media_use.pdf

Vanclooster, S., Bissell, S., van Eeghen, A. M., Chambers, N., De Waele, L., Byars, A. W., Capal, J. K., Cukier, S., Davis, P., Flinn, J., Gardner-Lubbe, S., Gipson, T., Heunis, T. M., Hook, D., Kingswood, J. C., Krueger, D. A., Kumm, A. J., Sahin, M., Schoeters, E., . . . de Vries, P. J. (2022). The research landscape of tuberous sclerosis complex–associated neuropsychiatric disorders (TAND): A comprehensive scoping review. *Journal of Neurodevelopmental Disorders*, *14*(1), 13. https://doi.org/10.1186/s11689-022-09423-3

Vanderbilt Kennedy Center. (2021a). *Healthy bodies boys. A parent's guide on puberty for boys with disabilities.* https://www.rwjbh.org/documents/csh/Healthy-Bodies-for-Boys-A-Parent-s-Guide-on-Puberty-for-Boys-with-Disabilities-English.pdf

Vanderbilt Kennedy Center. (2021b). *Health bodies girls. A parent's guide on puberty for girls with disabilities.* https://www.rwjbh.org/documents/csh/Healthy-Bodies-for-Girls-A-Parent-s-Guide-on-Puberty-for-Girls-with-Disabilities-English.pdf

Van Schalkwyk, G. I., Marin, C. E., Ortiz, M., Rolison, M., Qayyum, Z., McPartland, J. C., Lebowitz, E. R., Volkmar, F. R., & Silverman, W. K. (2017). Social media use, friendship quality, and the moderating role of anxiety in adolescents with autism spectrum disorder. *Journal of Autism and Developmental Disorders*, *47*(9), 2805–2813. https://doi.org/10.1007/s10803-017-3201-6

Von Gontard, A., Hussong, J., Yang, S. S., Chase, J., Franco, I., & Wright, A. (2022). Neurodevelopmental disorders and incontinence in children and adolescents: Attention-deficit/hyperactivity disorder, autism spectrum disorder, and intellectual disability—a consensus document of the International Children's Continence Society. *Neurourology and Urodynamics*, *41*(1), 102–114. https://doi.org/10.1002/nau.24798

Wang, S., Wang, B., Drury, V., Drake, S., Sun, N., Alkhairo, H., Arbelaez, J., Duhn, C., Tourette International Collaborative Genetics (TIC Genetics), Bal, V. H., Langley, K., Martin, J., Hoekstra, P. J., Dietrich, A., Xing, J., Heiman, G. A., Tischfield, J. A., Fernandez, T. V., Owen, M. J., O'Donovan, M. C., ... Willsey, A. J. (2023). Rare X-linked variants carry predominantly male risk in autism, Tourette syndrome, and ADHD. *Nature Communications*, *14*(1), 8077. https://doi.org/10.1038/s41467-023-43776-0

Warrier, V., Greenberg, D. M., Weir, E., Buckingham, C., Smith, P., Lai, M. C., Allison, C., & Baron-Cohen, S. (2020). Elevated rates of autism, other neurodevelopmental and psychiatric diagnoses, and autistic traits in transgender and gender-diverse individuals. *Nature Communications*, *11*(1), 3959. https://doi.org/10.1038/s41467-020-17794-1

Wigham, S., Rodgers, J., South, M., McConachie, H., & Freeston, M. (2015). The interplay between sensory processing abnormalities, intolerance of uncertainty, anxiety and restricted and repetitive behaviours in autism spectrum disorder. *Journal of Autism and Developmental Disorders*, *45*(4), 943–952. https://doi.org/10.1007/s10803-014-2248-x

Williams, K. *Laxative safety: Miralax and autism.* Online at Autism Speaks https://www.autismspeaks.org/expert-opinion/miralax-autism

Willsey, H. R., Willsey, A. J., Wang, B., & State, M. W. (2022). Genomics, convergent neuroscience and progress in understanding autism spectrum disorder. *Nature Reviews: Neuroscience, 23*(6), 323–341. https://doi.org/10.1038/s41583-022-00576-7

Winder-Patel, B., Tudor, M. E., Kerns, C. M., Davis, K., Nordahl, C. W., Amaral, D. G., & Solomon, M. (2022). Often undiagnosed but treatable: Case vignettes and clinical considerations for assessing anxiety disorders in youth with autism spectrum disorder and intellectual disability. *Evidence-based Practice in Child and Adolescent Mental Health, 7*(1), 24–40. https://doi.org/10.1080/23794925.2021.1923090

Winter, A. S., Fountain, C., Cheslack-Postava, K., & Bearman, P. S. (2020). The social patterning of autism diagnoses reversed in California between 1992 and 2018. *Proceedings of the National Academy of Sciences of the United States of America, 117*(48), 30295–30302. https://doi.org/10.1073/pnas.2015762117

Wolicki, S. B., Bitsko, R. H., Danielson, M. L., Holbrook, J. R., Zablotsky, B., Walkup, J. T., Woods, D. W., & Mink, J. W. (2019). Children with Tourette syndrome in the United States: Parent-reported diagnosis, co-occurring disorders, severity, and influence of activities on Tics. *Journal of Developmental and Behavioral Pediatrics : JDBP, 40*(6), 407–414. https://doi.org/10.1097/DBP.0000000000000667 Copy Download .nbib Format:

Woodbury-Smith, M. R., Loftin, R., Westphal, A., & Volkmar, F. R. (2022). Vulnerability to ideologically-motivated violence among individuals with autism spectrum disorder. *Frontiers in Psychiatry, 13*, 873121. https://doi.org/10.3389/fpsyt.2022.873121

Xie, F., Pascual, E., & Oakley, T. (2023). Functional echolalia in autism speech: Verbal formulae and repeated prior utterances as communicative and cognitive strategies. *Frontiers in Psychology, 14*, 1010615. https://doi.org/10.3389/fpsyg.2023.1010615

Xie, S., Karlsson, H., Dalman, C., Widman, L., Rai, D., Gardner, R. M., Magnusson, C., Schendel, D. E., Newschaffer, C. J., & Lee, B. K. (2019). Family history of mental and neurological disorders and risk of autism. *JAMA Network Open, 2*(3), e190154. https://doi.org/10.1001/jamanetworkopen.2019.0154

Young, S., & Cocallis, K. (2023). A systematic review of the relationship between neurodiversity and psychosexual functioning in individuals with autism spectrum disorder (ASD) or attention-deficit/hyperactivity disorder (ADHD). *Neuropsychiatric Disease and Treatment, 19*, 1379–1395. https://doi.org/10.2147/NDT.S319980

Zahra, A., Wang, Y., Wang, Q., & Wu, J. (2022). Shared etiology in autism spectrum disorder and epilepsy with functional disability. *Behavioural Neurology, 2022*, 5893519. https://doi.org/10.1155/2022/5893519

Index

For the benefit of digital users, indexed terms that span two pages (e.g., 52–53) may, on occasion, appear on only one of those pages.

Note: Boxes are indicated by an italic b following the page number.

ableism, 24
academic demands, 35–36
adolescent autism
  case studies, 11–14
  causes and controversies, 24–25
  Criterion A, 17–19
  Criterion B, 19
  Criterion C, 19–20b
  Criterion D, 19–20b
  Criterion E, 19–20b
  diagnosis of, 14–18
  diagnostic criteria for, 18–20
  diagnostic delay in, 21–22
  gender identity and, 26–27
  introduction to, 2–3, 9–10
  key experiences, 10
  prevalence of, 22–23
Affordable Care Act (ACA), 177
air pollution factors, 25
Americans With Disabilities Act (ADA), 51–52, 177
anxiety
  adolescent autism and, 11–12
  disorders, 56, 63, 80–81, 86–87, 89–94
  introduction to, 4–5
  social connections and, 116b
applied behavioral analysis (ABA), 121
aromantic, 169–170
asexuality, 6–7, 167, 169–170, 202
Asperger's disorder, 15–16
attention deficit/hyperactivity disorder (ADHD)
  co-occurring, 80–85, 98–101
  diagnosing, 61
  dual diagnosis with, 49
  gender differences, 62b
  introduction to, 4–5
augmentative and alternative communication, 12, 40b, 142
Autistic Self Advocacy Network (ASAN), 51–52, 157, 175–176, 181, 191–192, 196
avoidant-restrictive food intake disorder (ARFID), 101–102

bedwetting (nocturnal enuresis), 76–78
birth control, 149b
borderline personality disorder, 81–84

229

brain development, 24–25, 64–65
breast development, 144–145
broad autism phenotype, 24
bullying, 5, 95, 106, 108, 111, 124, 126–129

Center on Secondary Education for Students With Autism Spectrum Disorder, 45
classroom support, 36–40
cognitive testing, 33–34, 82, 87
college for young autistic adults, 196–198
Common Sense Media, 166–167
comorbidity, 26
concrete instructions, 40–41, 43
connective tissue disorders, 25–26, 57–58, 67–69, 71, 76, 86
co-occurring genetic conditions
  case studies, 77–78
  connective tissue disorders, 26, 56–57, 69, 70–73, 76, 86
  epilepsy, 4, 25–26, 62b, 56, 63–64, 69, 73–75
  fragile X syndrome (FXS), 56–58, 63–67
  hypermobility spectrum disorders, 67–69b
  tuberous sclerosis complex (TSC), 63–67, 76
co-occurring medical conditions
  in adolescent autism, 25–26
  diagnostic overshadowing, 57–60b, 62–63, 68
  Ehlers-Danlos syndrome (EDS), 63–64, 67–68
  gastrointestinal (GI) disorders, 4, 25–26, 63–64, 70–73, 100–101
  gender differences, 62b
  intellectual disability, 4, 25–26, 56, 63, 65, 67, 73–75
  introduction to, 4, 56–58
co-occurring mental health conditions
  ADHD, 80–85, 98–101
  in adolescent autism, 25–26
  case studies, 81–84, 87–98
  depression, 84–86, 88–89, 95b, 94–98
  diagnostic overshadowing, 4, 84
  disordered eating, 101–103

  eating disorders, 4–5, 61, 80–81, 86, 96, 98–99, 101–103
  gender differences, 80
  intellectual disability, 4, 80, 87–95b, 95, 99, 100b
  introduction to, 4–5, 80–81
  obsessive compulsive disorder (OCD), 81, 84, 91b
  self-injury, 81–84
  sleep disturbances, 80–81, 98–99, 103–104
  suicidality, 81–82, 98b
  tic disorder, 81, 91b
  violent behavior, 104
coping strategies, 43–44
counterfeit deviance, 165
Crehan, Eileen, 165–166
Criterion A, 17–19
Criterion B, 19
Criterion C, 19–20b,
Criterion D, 19–20b,
Criterion E, 19–20b
cyberbullying, 128–129

dating, 124–126
deficit model, 53
depression, 4–5, 11–12, 95b, 84–86, 88–89, 94–98
developmental delays, 65, 69, 197
Diagnostic and Statistical Manual of Mental Disorders (DSM-5), 15–17, 86–87
Diagnostic Manual—Intellectual Disability, 90
diagnostic overshadowing, 4, 57–60b, 62–63, 68, 84
digital assisted communication, 13
direct communication, 125–126, 171
disordered eating, 101–103
driving skills, 199–200
dual diagnosis, 49

eating disorders, 4–5, 61, 80–81, 86, 96, 98–99, 101–103
echolalia, 19, 38–39, 87, 91
Ehlers–Danlos syndrome (EDS), 63–64, 67–68

Index

Eliot-Pearson Department of Child Study & Human Development, 165
employment for young autistic adults, 194–196
empowerment, 157–158, 187–188
environmental factors, 24–25, 31, 73–74, 139
epilepsy, 4, 25–26, 62b, 56, 63–69, 73–75
erections, 143–144
estrogen changes, 138
externalizing behaviors, 96
extracurricular activities, 106, 118, 119, 127, 130

Federal Education Right to Privacy Act (FERPA), 177
fragile X primary ovarian insufficiency (FXPOI), 65–66
fragile X syndrome (FXS), 56–58, 63–67
fragile X tremor-ataxia syndrome, 65
friendships, 109–118

gastrointestinal (GI) disorders, 4, 25–26, 63–64, 70–73, 100–101
gender-affirming care, 141, 168–169
gender differences
  in ADHD, 62b
  in autism, 57–58
  co-occurring medical conditions, 62b
  in epilepsy, 73–74
  intellectual disability, 117
  social connections and, 117b
  urological disorders, 75–79
gender dysphoria, 141b, 142–143, 168
gender identity
  adolescent autism and, 26–27
  gender-queer persons, 26
  nonbinary persons, 26, 117, 168
  overview of, 167–170
  transgender persons, 6–7, 26, 141, 167, 202
gender-queer persons, 26
generalized anxiety disorder, 86–87
gonadal changes, 138, 142
Grandin, Temple, 92
guardianship, 190–191

healthcare, 200–202
Health Insurance Portability and Accountability Act (HIPAA), 177
healthy sexuality, 155
helicopter parenting, 12
high functioning, 31, 101
homeschooling, 11–12, 36b, 134
hormonal changes, 136–137b, 138, 142, 144, 149b, 169
housing for young autistic adults, 192–194
hygiene routines, 137, 149–151
hypermobility spectrum disorders, 67–69b

Individualized Education Program (IEP)
  as formal support, 3–4
  in secondary school, 30, 45–50
  Section 504 of the Rehabilitation Act (1973), 47–50
  transition to adulthood, 176–177, 182, 184, 187
Individuals With Disabilities Education Act (IDEA), 48, 177
infantilization, 168
intellectual ability, 32, 95b, 127
intellectual disability
  bullying and, 126
  co-occurring, 4, 25–26, 56, 63, 65, 67, 73–75, 95b, 80, 87–95, 99, 100b
  gender differences, 117
  IQ scores, 33
  prevalence, 22–23
  sex-related education and, 153, 156, 165
intelligence quotient (IQ), 21–22, 31–34
internalizing disorders, 96
International Classification of Diseases, 89
intersex persons, 6–7, 24–25, 202
iPad use, 12–13

least restrictive environment, 44–45, 48–49, 134, 177
LGBTQIA+ persons
  asexuality, 6–7, 167, 169–170, 202
  gender-affirming care, 141, 168–169
  gender dysphoria, 141b, 142–143, 168
  intersex persons, 6–7, 24–25, 202
  introduction to, 6–7
  nonbinary persons, 26, 117, 168

LGBTQIA+ persons (*Continued*)
  queerness, 6–7, 26, 162, 167, 202
  sexual orientation, 167–170
  transgender persons, 6–7, 26, 141, 167, 202
low functioning, 101

marginalization., 167–168
masturbation, 170–171
media and internet, 165–167
medical conditions. *See* co-occurring medical conditions
menstruation changes, 137–149
mental health conditions. *See* co-occurring mental health conditions
migraines, 11–12
monetary management, 199
monotropism, 53–54
mood disorders, 4, 61, 63, 65–66, 80–81, 95

National Autistic Society (UK), 13
National Resource Center for Supported Decision- Making, 190–191
neurodevelopment, 24–26
neurodevelopmental conditions
  ADHD and, 85
  co-occurring conditions, 86
  cyberbullying and, 129
  in *DSM-5*, 17–18, 20
  OCD and, 91
  urinary issues and, 76
nocturnal emissions, 143–144
nocturnal enuresis (bedwetting), 76–78
nonbinary persons, 26, 117, 168
nonspeaking/nonverbal autistic people, 10, 12–13, 17, 18, 36, 57, 61, 71, 87, 90, 95, 96, 127–128, 132, 153, 156
nonverbal communication, 10, 17, 18, 132

obsessive compulsive disorder (OCD), 81, 84, 91*b*
Office of Disability Services Innovation, 179
Office of Independent Living Programs, 179
Office of Intellectual and Developmental Disability, 179
off-label recommendations, 58
Olmstead v. L.C. (1999), 193–194
online multiplayer games, 106, 129
oppositional defiant disorder, 84

paraphilic sexual interests, 164
Parent Training and Information Centers, 51
pedophilia, 164
peer buddy programs, 122–123
peer groups, 121–122
person-first language, 27
PLAY IT SAFE (Center on Secondary Education for Students With Autism Spectrum Disorder), 133
pornography, 166
predictable spaces, 40–42
profound autism, 100*b*
Program for the Education and Enrichment of Relational Skills (PEERS), 122–123, 126–127
Proloquo2Go app, 13
puberty. *See also* sexuality and puberty
  birth control, 149*b*
  changes in, 137–141
  clinician choice, 137*b*
  hormonal changes, 136–137*b*, 138, 142, 144, 149*b*, 169
  hygiene routines, 149–151
  introduction to, 6–7, 136–137, 152–154
  menstruation changes, 137–149
  preparing for, 141–143

queerness, 6–7, 26, 162, 167, 202
quiet spaces, 43

Real Education and Access for Healthy Youth Act, 157
Reichow, Brian, 16
repetitive behaviors, 23, 66, 81, 87, 91, 128
repetitive motor movements, 19
restricted interests, 19

routines, 40–41, 43, 46, 49, 70, 72, 83, 87, 92–94, 103–104, 137, 149–151

schizophrenia spectrum, 61, 80–81
school size, 134*b*
secondary school autism
   academic demands, 35–36
   case studies, 30, 33, 37
   classroom support, 36–40
   concerns about abuse, 52*b*
   coping strategies, 43–44
   introduction to, 3–4, 29–31
   parental connections and, 44–46
   shifting changes in, 31–35
   social demands, 35–36
   strengths-based approach to education, 53–55
   success strategies, 40–42
   transition plan, 50–53
   universal design and, 44*b*
Section 504 of the Rehabilitation Act (1973), 47–50, 177
self-advocacy, 7–8, 175, 176, 184–185, 190, 191, 198
self-determination, 7–8, 134, 157, 159–160, 175–176, 179, 181–182, 184, 190–191, 197, 199, 201
self-injurious behavior (SIB), 87–94
self-injury, 81–84, 87
sensory breaks, 34–35
sensory overload, 43
services cliff, 189–190
severely affected, 31
sex education, 152, 156–157, 162
sex/sexuality education, 6–7, 152, 154–158, 162, 164–166, 172*b*
sexual abuse, 153, 155
sexual experiences, 171–172
sexuality and puberty. *See also* LGBTQIA+ persons
   boundaries, 162–163
   breast development, 144–145
   consent issues, 159–161
   erections, 143–144
   gender identity, 167–170
   healthy sexuality, 155
   masturbation, 170–171
   media and internet, 165–167
   nocturnal emissions, 143–144
   no means no, 159–162
   offenders, 163–165
   pornography, 166
   sensory considerations, 172*b*
   sex/sexuality education, 6–7, 152–158, 162, 164–166, 172*b*
   sexual experiences, 171–172
   sexual orientation, 167–170
   sexual victimization risk, 162*b*
sexual orientation, 167–170
sexual victimization risk, 162*b*
sleep disturbances, 80–81, 98–99, 103–104
SMART goals (specific, measurable, attainable, relevant, and time bound), 49, 182
social behaviors, 23, 29–30, 122
social communication, 10, 16–18, 20*b*, 53–54, 65, 68, 81, 85, 92, 100
social connections
   anxiety and, 116*b*
   autistic strengths and, 106
   bullying and, 126–129
   choosing classes, 123–124
   dating, 124–126
   extracurricular activities, 106, 118, 119, 127, 130
   friendships, 109–118
   gender differences and, 117*b*
   home life, 119–121
   introduction to, 5, 105–106
   logistics of, 113
   online multiplayer games, 106, 129
   peer buddy programs, 122–123
   peer groups, 121–122
   practicing, 113
   relationship nuances, 108*b*
   school size and, 134*b*
   social engineering, 39–40, 106, 110, 118–119, 121–122
   social media and, 128–135
   social thinker/social thinking, 5, 107–109, 113
   TV and movies, 115*b*
social demands, 35–36

Social Emotional NeuroScience Endocrinology Theatre, 124
social-emotional reciprocity, 17–18
social engineering, 39–40, 106, 110, 118–119, 121–122
social interactions in school, 36–40
social media, 5, 106, 112, 129–135, 165–166
Social Security Disability Insurance (SSDI), 180
social skills, 5, 95, 105–107, 110–111, 121, 122
social thinker/social thinking, 5, 107–109
Socio-Dramatic Affective-Relational Intervention, 124
speed dating, 121–122
Stanford's Neurodiversity Project, 53
stimming, 39, 74, 91
strengths-based approach to education, 53–55
suicidality, 81–82, 98*b*
Supplemental Security Income (SSI), 180, 194–195
supported decision-making, 191–192

technology use, 12–13
tic disorder, 81, 91*b*
transgender persons, 6–7, 26, 141, 167, 202
transition support team, 40–41
transition to adulthood
   case studies, 182
   college, 196–198
   driving, 199–200
   employment, 194–196
   guardianship, 190–191
   housing, 192–194
   introduction to, 7–8, 173–175
   legal planning, 192
   monetary management, 199
   parental roles, 185–188
   planning team, 188
   planning tools, 188
   preparation and planning, 181–184
   relevant laws, 176–179
   self-advocacy, 7–8, 175, 176, 184–185, 190, 191, 198
   self-determination, 7–8, 134, 157, 159–160, 175–176, 179, 181–182, 184, 190–191, 197, 199, 201
   service agencies, 179–181
   services cliff, 189–190
   supported decision-making, 191–192
   vocational rehabilitation, 179, 195
   wellness and healthcare, 200–202
trusted adults, 40–41, 126, 133
TSC-associated neuropsychiatric disorders (TAND), 64
tuberous sclerosis complex (TSC), 63–67, 76

universal design, 44*b*
The Unwritten Rules of Social Relationships (Grandin), 92
urinary incontinence, 76–77
urological disorders, 75–79
urotherapy, 78
U.S. Centers for Disease Control and Prevention (CDC), 22–23
U.S. Department of Education, 179
U.S. Department of Education Office for Civil Rights, 48
U.S. Department of Health and Human Services, 193–194
U.S. Food and Drug Administration, 58, 72
U.S. Interagency Autism Coordinating Committee, 180
U.S. Office for Civil Rights, 52–53

vesicoureteral reflux, 76
video games, 54, 202
violent behavior, 104
vocational rehabilitation, 179, 195
Volkmar, Fred, 16

World Health Organization (WHO), 89